F-19 Stealth Air Combat

F-19 Stealth
Air Combat

Pete Bonanni

**Silicon
Valley**

Osborne **McGraw-Hill**
2600 Tenth Street
Berkeley, California 94710
U.S.A.

Osborne McGraw-Hill offers software for sale. For information on software, translations, or book distributors outside of the U.S.A., please write to Osborne **McGraw-Hill** at the above address.

This book is printed on recycled paper.

F-19 Stealth Air Combat

1234567890 DOC 99876543210

ISBN 0-07-881655-6

Acquisitions Editor: Roger Stewart
Associate Editor: Laurie Beaulieu
Technical Reviewer: Robert Bonanni
Copy Editor: Ann Krueger-Spivack
Proofreader: Julie Anjos
Word Processors: Judy Koplan, Stefany Otis, Linda Higham
Book Design: Judy Wohlfrom
Production Supervisor: Kevin Shafer

This book was produced using Ventura Publisher Version 2. Cover art by Steven Black Design, Inc. Cover illustration courtesy of the Department of Defense. Color supplier, Phoenix Color Corp.

Dedication

To Teresa

Contents

Stealth—The Ghost of the Air

Several years ago, I was the commander of an F-16 squadron, the 61st Tactical Fighter Squadron, based out of MacDill Air Force Base in Florida. The mission of the squadron was to train pilots transitioning from other aircraft into the "Electric Jet," the F-16 (its nickname came from its "fly-by-wire" computer controlled electrical flight control system). One of the transitioning pilots on his way to Korea was none other than Pete Bonanni, the author of *Falcon Air Combat*. I remember him well in that he was a prototypical fighter pilot: confident, bold, brash, with a "can-do" attitude. He was an excellent pilot with a gift for teaching the others what he had learned and experienced. Like his first book, *F-19 Stealth Air Combat* is again an outstanding blend of "how to" and aircraft tactical applications.

In Chapter 2, Pete describes a typical mission that was played out many times in Vietnam. As I read the story, my heartbeat increased, the hair on the back of my head stood at attention, and sweat began to form on my brow. (Well not really, since fighter pilots are always cool, calm and under complete control.) It is said that fighter pilots can never tell a story without using their hands to describe the fight—on any base in the Air Force, on any given day, the hands describe the action. Well, you can imagine what my hands were saying as I recalled and described to Pete an air-to-air engagement in North Vietnam with a MiG over downtown Hanoi similar to the experience he relays to you. Prior to the engagement, the flak from groundfire was so thick that you could get out of your aircraft and walk on it; SAMs (Surface-to-Air Missiles) whizzed by the canopy and you instinctively ducked because they were so close. It was during one of these engagements when the enemy was getting a little too close that I silently prayed to be invisible to the radar controlled guns and missiles. Little did I know that I was praying for Stealth...the jargon of today. Nor did I know that several years later I would have the honor to serve my country as one of the first Stealth fighter pilots flying the top-secret F-117 designed to exploit low-observable stealth technology.

Contrary to recent press releases, the F-117 program was one of the best kept secrets in the history of the United States. The aircraft was operational many years before its existence was even speculated about. During the first briefing I received on the aircraft, I can recall thinking it would never fly. "This must be a joke," I thought to myself, "no aircraft with all these flat surfaces could possibly fly." It looked like something from *Star Wars* (see the front cover). But I was soon to learn that fly it did, with the ease and grace of any aircraft I had flown. It used proven computer controlled fly-by-wire technology which allowed this bizarre aircraft to take advantage of its stealthy characteristics and yet be maneuverable. It was conceived and built by the Lockheed Advanced Development Projects or the famous "Skunk Works." In essence it is a single-seat fighter designed to penetrate threat environments and attack high-value targets with pinpoint accuracy. Pete describes very nicely in Chapter 2 the F-117 as reported by the press. I wish I could tell you more about the amazing aircraft and its flying characteristics but as the saying goes, "someday the world will know, and when it does, Americans will be proud to have this aircraft on their side." American technology does it again, forcing our enemies to think twice before challenging us in combat. Can you imagine what it would be like to operate with relative impunity against your enemy? It's like getting into a boxing ring against an opponent who can't see you; for our opponents, it's like trying to protect themselves against a ghost.

I have had fun playing this game and reliving my glory days—now it's your turn. Take Pete's instructions in this excellent book, and play an aircraft simulation game that will test your flying abilities and hone your Stealth fighter pilot skills. Check Six and may all your bombs be "shacks" (that's fighter pilot jargon for watch out for aircraft behind you and put your bombs right on target).

Milan "Viper" Zimer

Vice Commander/Inspector General, the 24th Composite Wing, Howard AFB, Panama
Flight Commander with more than 400 hours of flight combat, and more than 3,600 flying hours
Flew more than 100 combat missions to North Vietnam in the F-4C
Flew more than 80 combat missions in the F-4D/E
Served as Wing Executive Officer, Chief of Protocol, 31st Tactical
Fighter Wing, Homestead AFB, Florida
Distinguished Flying Cross with four oak leaf clusters, the Meritorious Service Medal with one oak
leaf cluster, Air Medal with 19 oak leaf clusters, Commendation Medal
with three oak leaf clusters, and the Combat Readiness Medal
Promoted to the grade of colonel Oct. 1, 1982
Currently: Director for Mission Planning Systems, Lockheed Sanders, and working on the
Advanced Tactical Fighter F-22

Introduction

The F-19 simulation provides the pilot a unique chance to experience a new chapter in air warfare. The simulation creates high-tempo air combat operations in a *low-observable* (LO) aircraft, the F-19. The F-19 features a drastically reduced radar and IR profile that make it difficult to detect by the enemy. Along with these stealth features, the F-19 is equipped with a suite of modern avionics and weapons. Opposing the F-19 pilot in the simulation are modern air defense systems consisting of Surface-to-Air Missiles (SAMs) and enemy fighters. In order to master the complex *tactical environment* created by the simulation, the F-19 pilot must develop a corresponding *tactical perspective*.

This book will give the F-19 pilot a knowledge base to build a tactical perspective. Very specific procedures and fighter pilot rules of thumb are covered in order to build a solid foundation in F-19 fighter tactics. The instruction in *F-19 Stealth Air Combat* is given from a fighter pilot's perspective. The reader will gain insight into modern fighter weapons and tactics and how they relate to employing an LO fighter such as the F-19. Along with specific "how to" instruction, I have included several stories (most from my own experiences) to illustrate key points along the way. Again, this book strives to build the reader's tactical fighter perspective in order to help him or her fight and win in F-19 stealth air combat.

All of my sorties in the F-19 simulation were flown using an IBM AT computer. All of the screen shots in this book and references to specific keys are based on this same computer.

Pete Bonanni

1

BATTLE FOR THE HIGH GROUND

"The sky, too, is to become another battlefield,
no less important than the battlefields of land
and sea."
—Giulio Douhet
Prophet of air power

The sun slowly sets in the west, and the light fades along with your fears. The hours of sunlight are very dangerous; they're ruled by Falcons, Eagles, Fulcrums, and Flankers—the daylight predators. The night, however, gives birth to a different set of survival rules. Power and maneuverability are no longer the most important fighter attributes when darkness falls. At night, concealment becomes the key to success. Your jet is the first operational fighter designed for concealment from the ground up. Tonight's mission will test these features along with your night fighting skills.

The terrorist leader who brought down a U.S. commercial 747 has been identified, and intelligence has finally tracked him down. Tonight he will be flying on a heavily guarded military transport. Your mission is to hit the transport, and see that he gets the thrill of a 30,000 free-fall (sans parachute). In order to accomplish this, you will have to slip past ground-based acquisition radars and escort fighters, shoot down the transport, and slip away into the night. An impossible mission for a "muscle" fighter, but a perfect job for your jet.

You take the runway, run up the power, and check the instruments one last time before takeoff. The blinding glare of the runway lights stretches out in front of you, pointing the way into blackness. You release the brakes and bring the throttle to full power—the acceleration is smooth but does not inspire confidence. The lack of thrust in this jet is still hard to get used to but you finally get airborne, suck the gear up, and turn toward the ocean. With the runway lights at six o'clock and nothing but ocean below, the jet is swallowed up by the night.

This is not a classic fighter engagement of large aircraft formations and high *G* maneuvers; instead you are entering a fight of careful planning and single-ship execution. The rules are simple. Avoid detection and ambush the enemy before they find and kill you. Your passive infrared and radar sensors probe the night as you fly out to meet the enemy. U.S. technology has given you the edge, but it is a slim one. Going feet dry, the coastline slips past at 800 feet per second as you enter the solitary and deadly world of Stealth Air Combat.

SOUND AND FURY

Surprisingly, this form of warfare is not new. Radar-evading stealth technology is just the latest move in the contest between attacking aircraft and defensive forces that spans the history of aerial combat. The F-19

Figure 1-1. WW I fighter

simulation re-creates a modern combat environment of fighter versus defender, but even the vaunted low- observable technology embodied in the Stealth Fighter does not end the game. Attempts to defend and control airspace over friendly lines has been going on since the beginning of air combat and will continue into the future.

The seeds of modern air combat were planted in the First World War as aircraft developed into bombing and reconnaissance platforms. To stop the enemy from performing these missions, air-to-air combat soon emerged along with ground-based Anti-Aircraft Artillery (AAA). From the outset, aircraft proved far more successful at countering other aircraft than ground based defenses. Air-to-air fighter aircraft, like the one shown in Figure 1-1, became the single most important means of controlling the skies. In World War I, control of the sky (also called *air superiority*) allowed your side to perform reconnaissance and the offensive missions of bombing and *strafing* the enemy and denied these same missions to your opponents.

Fighter Aircraft

Fighter aircraft of both sides had an uphill struggle to gain air superiority in World War I. Neither side gained complete control of the skies. This was not only because the combatants were evenly matched but also due to the limitations of fighter aircraft themselves.

In order to shoot down another aircraft, you first have to detect the target, then close on your adversary and achieve weapons parameters. This proved to be no easy task in a fabric covered bi-plane with a fixed aiming sight and a machine-gun. Finding the enemy was accomplished by flying a visual search pattern that amounted to wandering around the skies until you blundered into the bad guys (a visual air-to-air search is similar to a blind squirrel searching for an acorn). Once you gained a tally (sighted the enemy), you had to close within a few hundred feet for a difficult machine-gun shot on a very uncooperative target. While the task of shooting down another aircraft was far from impossible, finding the enemy visually on a large battlefield was hit or miss, and aerial engagements were time-consuming and often inconclusive. When you add to this the limited range and endurance of these early fighters, it is easy to see why defending friendly territory and gaining air superiority was so difficult.

Anti-Aircraft Artillery

AAA (pronounced "triple A") was not as effective as fighter aircraft at shooting down enemy aircraft, but Anti-Aircraft Artillery had the advantage of being more responsive. When the skies are filled with enemy aircraft and all the fighter pilots on your side are in the bar, at least you have some protection in the form of AAA.

In addition, defenders could mass AAA guns around a valuable target, discouraging would-be attackers. AAA gunners, like fighter pilots, relied primarily on finding their targets visually and had the additional problem of air defense guns with relatively low muzzle velocities and firing rates. This made hitting a maneuvering aircraft difficult and led to the primary AAA tactic of World War I, barrage fire. In *barrage fire* the guns were fired up into a sector of the sky where the aircraft would pass. This form of AAA engagement could be effective without actually shooting down enemy aircraft by keeping would-be attackers away from critical target areas or making them miss if they did press the attack. Despite this partially successful tactic, aircraft flying air-to-ground missions still held a clear advantage and usually emerged unscathed from AAA defended targets.

The limitations in defensive forces embodied in the air-to-air fighter and AAA gun could have made offensive air power a decisive factor in the war had it not been for a corresponding wide range of shortcomings in aircraft in general. *Offensive air power* (for our purposes) is the destruction of enemy ground forces by aircraft. The airplane during World War I did not possess the payload or range to be an effective offensive weapon. Even though bombers and fighters flying ground-attack missions did make a contribution to the war efforts of both sides, this contribution was minor. The math was simply not there. One hundred World War II bomber sorties could carry approximately one million pounds of bombs 1000 miles to their targets while 100 World War I bomber sorties could barely carry 200,000 pounds over 300 miles. There simply was not enough aircraft available during World War I with sufficient range and payload capability to destroy important targets.

The air war in World War I has been described as a lot of "sound and fury, signifying nothing." This may be true in terms of the direct impact of air power on the war's outcome but it is clearly false in terms of lessons learned for future conflicts. World War I gave men of vision a glimpse of the future importance of air power. With this knowledge, air forces were created that proved to be decisive in the next war.

THE *OSTFRIESLAND* GOES DOWN

Between World War I and II, aircraft capabilities grew steadily as did supporting organizations and air doctrine. Although progress was made there were casualties along the way. The most noted of these was an Army officer named Billy Mitchell. A major proponent of air power, Billy Mitchell commanded air forces in World War I and had seen firsthand the promise of air power.

A Test for Air Power

Mitchell returned to the U.S. filled with new ideas for implementing air power, and immediately ran afoul of the established military leadership. Billy Mitchell's fatal flaw was that he wanted a fundamental change in military force structure at a pace that could not be achieved. Billy Mitchell advocated an Air Service branch separate from the Army and Navy. He wanted this new branch of the military to take over the Navy's role of protecting the U.S. coasts. These ideas were based on the premise that the airplane could be used as an offensive weapon and could not be effectively countered.

Billy Mitchell's case for air power met with open skepticism, and with good reason. Air power had made its debut in the last war with much fanfare but little substance. The military brass, caught between the wars with shrinking budgets, did not want to make sweeping changes in military force structure based upon unproven theories of air power. Mitchell did not let up, however, and finally Congress authorized a test of air power that took place in June of 1921.

The test was simple and direct. Several captured German war ships would be used as targets, and Mitchell's bombers and similar Navy aircraft would attack them. The targets would be attacked, one by one, in a controlled bombing range environment. After each attack, Navy observers would assess the damage to the target ships and signal for the attack to continue.

The first test subject was a submarine that was attacked by Navy aircraft. Several bombs were dropped on the first pass, all of them missing the target. The Navy bombers found the range on the second pass and scored direct hits, sending the sub to the bottom within minutes.

Next up were Billy Mitchell's Army Martin bombers, shown in Figure 1-2. This time the target was a destroyer. Military and civilian leaders watched from a nearby ship while Mitchell's pilots sunk the ship in less than 20 minutes. The German light cruiser *Frankfort* was next on card, and again the Army Martins, dropping 600lb bombs, finished the ship in quick fashion. It's hard to fathom, but there were Naval officers who observed all of these attacks and still believed that Mitchell's aircraft could not sink the battleship *Ostfriesland,* the last target ship in the test. They pointed out to the press that these ships were not as well armored as a

Figure 1-2.   Martin bomber

battleship and thus the test so far had proved nothing. If Billy Mitchell could not sink the *Ostfriesland*, the Navy's outmoded "battleship" mentality would be reinforced and his theories of air power discredited.

The weather on the day scheduled for the *Ostfriesland* attack was miserable. High winds and low clouds almost canceled the test but Mitchell's bombers, along with the Navy aircraft, made a brief attack against the ship with 600lb bombs only to abort the attack due to bad weather. A post-attack inspection of the ship showed that this limited attack had killed a lot of fish, but left the target unharmed. The next day had good flying weather, and the attack on the *Ostfriesland* began again in earnest. On the first attack by Mitchell's pilots, the *Ostfriesland* was hit by a 1100lb bomb. The Navy range officer signaled for a halt in the action so the ship could be inspected, but before the order was carried out several more of the big bombs made contact. The Navy officers running the test were livid, but there was nothing that they could do. Inspection of the ship revealed a mass of twisted metal but, surprisingly, the *Ostfriesland* was ruled seaworthy. The Martin bombers dropped their remaining bombs into the empty ocean and went back to rearm. Seven bombers reappeared in the target area two hours later armed with only one bomb each—massive 2000lb bombs.

A New Era Begins

The first big bomb dropped had a delayed fuze and exploded beneath the battleship. The great ship keeled over from the effect of the undersea explosion and, as if to resist history itself, uprighted itself. Within moments, Mitchell's bombers were on the attack again, and scored six more hits in rapid succession. The onslaught was too much for the *Ostfriesland*. With a gaping hole visible in her hull, she rolled over and sank to the bottom. The final attack had taken only 20 minutes. With a worldwide audience watching, including several Navy Admirals who wept like babies, Mitch-ell's bombers ushered in the age of offensive air power. Despite this awesome demonstration, it would take several more years for the military bureaucracies to accept the results of this test and make changes.

The slow pace of U.S. acceptance of air power was too much for Billy Mitchell, and as time passed he became more and more outspoken. Eventually he was court-martialed and found guilty of insubordination and gradually faded from the public eye. History, of course, overturned the guilty verdict. Years later I had the pleasure of eating many a greasy hamburger in the dining hall at the U.S. Air Force Academy that bears Mitchell's name.

THE WIZARD WARS

Billy Mitchell did not dash his career on the rocks of the military bureaucracy in vain. All of his ideas were eventually embraced, and supporting doctrine and military force structure created. During the 1930s, the U.S. developed heavy bombers and carrier-based aircraft that became key combat assets in World War II. As the predicted offensive potential of aircraft became reality, the see-saw struggle that began in World War I between attackers and defenders took on greater intensity.

Success for the Offense

U.S. involvement in World War II started with a violent display of air power. The Japanese, showing the innovation and daring that would one day help them conquer automobile and consumer electronic markets around the globe, executed a "dastardly" attack against the U.S. Pacific fleet at Pearl Harbor. The American defenders were ill prepared and suffered heavy losses.

Offensive air power also produced similar results in the first years of the war in Europe. German armies, using supporting attack aircraft, had sliced across the continent and changed the face of Europe. Britain stood defiant after the fall of France, but had lost her foothold in Northern Europe and was unable to project power against the Germans. The English Channel separated the two ground armies, and without air superiority, the Germans could not attempt a channel crossing. The stage was set for a battle in the skies.

The Defenders Counter

The Battle of Britain was a fight for air superiority over Britain and the English Channel. It was the first decisive air battle in history and a clear victory for defensive air power. The German Luftwaffe failed to destroy the Royal Air Force, and Hitler's plans for lunch at Buckingham Palace were put on hold indefinitely.

The Luftwaffe was ill-equipped for this battle, and again the "math" drove the outcome. In an offensive air campaign the number of targets that need to be destroyed determines the bomb tonnage that must be carried and delivered. The Germans were trying to destroy the British Royal Air Force in the air and on the ground. Destroying the RAF in the air was next to impossible given the short legs of the German fighters and the long distance they had to fly. It was left to the bombers with supporting escorting fighters to do the job. The bombers used for the operation, though, were too few and too small to deliver a knockout blow, while the British defenses, fighting over friendly territory, made the Germans pay a heavy price for crossing the channel. The Luftwaffe did not inflict enough damage on the British in relation to the losses they suffered, so "to conclude, the victory fell on us" ("us" being the Allies). Offensive air power used by the Luftwaffe proved impotent in the face of strong fighter defenses during this stage of the war.

The Shrinking Sky

Scientists had found a counter to offensive aircraft, and it was used with divesting results in the Battle of Britain. Prior to the onset of war, a new technology emerged from the laboratories called RAdio Detecting And Ranging, or *radar*.

Radar served to shrink the airspace that was being defended, which made fighter aircraft more effective. Instead of taking off and roving the sky looking for the enemy, fighters could be left on the ground until an attack was detected by radar, and then vectored or steered toward the bombers. In effect, this allowed the defenders to shrink the sky and have fighter cover only where it was needed.

The RAF radar net proved very effective at performing this task. Use of the electronic spectrum to find and destroy the enemy began in World War II with the introduction of ground-based radars. This "wizard war," as it was later called, is still being fought today with the F-19 simulation replicating the latest, but not the last round in the struggle.

GÖRING'S IDLE BOAST

Bombers of the Royal Air Force faced a similar problem in trying to project power in the other direction across the English Channel. After the first British bombing raids, the Germans, who had also developed radar, built an extensive defensive radar network. This radar "fence" was called the *Kammhuber Line* after its builder, Major General Joseph Kammhuber, and stretched hundreds of miles across the attack routes used by the Allies.

This system consisted of overlapping box-shaped defensive zones called *himmelbetts* that were approximately 20 square miles in size. Each square possessed an Early Warning Radar with a range of over 70 miles and at least two Target Tracking Radars with an 18-mile range.

The Early Warning Radars fed information about large attacking bomber formations into a central control center that would then launch fighters and position them in front of the bomber cells. This technique was used primarily during daylight hours.

For night fighting, each individual himmelbett acted as a control center, directing their own attachment of night fighters. When enemy bombers appeared in their sector, the himmelbett would vector their assigned fighters into position using Target Tracking Radars. Me-110s, deadly German night fighters, were used to attack as singles, and after completing one attack the fighters would be directed toward another target.

The Kammhuber Line was a formidable defensive system, and Field Marshal Hermann Göring, the head of the Luftwaffe, claimed that if the allies ever bombed Berlin, "My name is Meyer" (a common Jewish name).

Countermeasures

This famous boast was based on the false premise of the "perfect defense." Mankind has been enamored with this idea since antiquity, and it has yet to be attained. There are always moves and countermoves in combat, and as the science of the World War II warring nations advanced, no force held the technological lead for very long. The RAF and then the American Army Air Corps did bomb Berlin and nearly every other German city but the road to Allied victory in the air was not smooth.

The British soon learned that they could not penetrate German airspace during daylight hours without taking unacceptable losses from the heavy concentrations of Luftwaffe fighters. At night, however, the RAF found that they could saturate the Kammhuber Line by massing their formations. Hundreds of attacking bombers would cross a small number of himmelbetts, completely overwhelming the defenders. The Germans countered by increasing the depth of the Kammhuber Line and soon this network covered thousands of square miles.

The British, undeterred by this change, introduced electronic warfare techniques that eventually seriously crippled the existing German defense network.

The Birth of Modern Electronic Warfare

Almost every electronic warfare (EW) technique that was applied in the night sky over Germany is still in use today. One of the first of these techniques introduced in World War II is called *intrusion jamming*. In this form of jamming the British attackers tuned in on the Luftwaffe radio frequencies used to direct enemy fighters. They then used German-speaking RAF personnel to issue false and confusing orders to the intercepting fighters. This of course caused great confusion and lost time as Luftwaffe fighter pilots flailed around the night sky trying to figure out who was who on the radio.

Another EW technique introduced was no doubt invented by a British scientist who had thick glasses, a slide ruler clipped to his belt, and a diabolical mind. This ingenious new EW technique went by the code "Window." Window, or *chaff* as it is now known, consists of strips of radar-reflective metal foil cut to specific lengths that correspond to the wavelength of the radar you intend to deceive. When dropped from aircraft, chaff reflects the radar energy the same way that an aircraft does, producing false targets. The more chaff dropped, the more targets created.

Chaff was used for the first time during an RAF raid on Hamburg. Over 700 British bombers crossed the channel in the raid, dropping chaff as they approached the German coast. Confusion swept the defenders as their radar scopes filled with targets. The 700 attacking bombers were lost in the thousands of blips that filled the radar screens along the Kammhuber line. It was the summer of 1943 and by this point in the war, radar was in widespread use on board night fighters as well as in terminal defenses around cities. Radar was used around the cities to guide searchlights and shoot AAA. Barrage fire was used by the AAA until the searchlights captured and illuminated a bomber. The AAA guns then switched to aimed fire to kill the target. On this night, the air defense radars did more harm than good as fighters and searchlights chased electronic phantoms amid the confused chatter of ground-based radar operators. With German defenses in disarray, the RAF pressed the attack on Hamburg. The city was struck hard and only a dozen aircraft were lost (a very low number for this type of raid).

In addition to chaff, the British also used bomber aircraft carrying active radar-jamming equipment called *Mandrel*. Mandrel was carried by two jamming aircraft and produced a signal that masked the incoming bomber raids. The British also broadcast a loud noise on the radio waves used by the Luftwaffe fighters with a voice jamming system called "Jostle." Intrusion, chaff, and active radar and voice jamming were used in various combinations throughout the war to keep the Luftwaffe off balance.

Victory in Europe

The Wizards waged a mighty war over Europe but what turned the tide in the air war had nothing to do with electronic subterfuge in the night sky. Instead, the Luftwaffe was brought to its knees by the direct application of American might. The U.S. finally developed fighters with enough range to escort bombers all the way to their targets. The P-51 Mustang, shown in Figure 1-3, could fly over 1,500 miles. Armed with this fighter, the U.S. took the fight deep into the heart of enemy territory. The German defense forces consisted of fighters and AAA guns, with fighters being the far more effective component. With the introduction of long-range escort fighters, enemy fighter defenses were countered, and the Allies gained air superiority over Europe.

AIR WAR OVER THE FROZEN CHOSEN

The pattern of electronic combat, countermeasures, and counter- counter measures was set in the night skies over Germany. Electronic combat was in an embryonic stage in this conflict but still contributed to the war efforts of both sides.

The air war in Korea was very similar to World War II in tactics, equipment, and the use of electronic warfare. This time it was U.S.-led

Figure 1-3.   P-51 Mustang

United Nations forces against Soviet-supported North Koreans and Chinese. Communist Air Defenses consisted of AAA sites and jet fighters.

The U.S. used the B-29 for strategic bombing and jet fighter-bombers for tactical targets. The B-29, shown in Figure 1-4, was a holdover from World War II but it still performed well in the Korean War. The big bombers first tried daylight bombing and were opposed by Russian-built MiG-15 fighters. They quickly switched to night bombing, EW, and escort fighters and negated the MiG-15. The F-86 fighters like the one shown in Figure 1-5 swept the skies of MiG-15s during the day when the radarless MiGs were the most effective, giving cover to U.S. fighter-bombers.

New Weapons for a Losing Cause

Soviet advisors tried to improve North Korean defenses and concentrated on AAA, since the best Russian fighter was already in use and was proving

Figure 1-4.   B-29 bomber

Figure 1-5.   F-86 Sabre

ineffective. They introduced the Soviet-built 100-mm gun along with radars to direct it.

In addition, the Russians introduced camouflage and dispersed sights in an effort to run a shell game and protect their AAA. Anti-Aircraft Artillery proved to be a far more successful air defense weapon in the Korean War than the MiG-15 fighter. AAA accounted for 544 USAF aircraft, more than five times the number of kills achieved by North Korean fighters. Although better than the fighter record, AAA could not stop the bomber onslaught, and the loss of the 544 aircraft shot down was minor when weighed against the hundreds of thousands of effective bombing sorties flown.

Losses to the Soviet radar-directed AAA guns were light due to U.S. active and passive jamming techniques. (*Passive jamming* refers to chaff and other forms of jamming that do not emit energy. *Active jamming* refers to electronic energy transmitted at target radar that degrades the reflective radar signal.) Since the Soviet gun-laying radars were built from imported German and American technology, the U.S. had little problem developing effective jamming techniques.

The Soviet radars tracked the incoming targets and fed range and airspeed information into computers that then output a firing solution. Instead of firing a barrage, the guns would be precisely aimed, and the target engaged.

Shooting AAA is very similar to duck hunting in that you must determine range and speed to know how much lead you must take on the target. In duck hunting you just "eyeball" the target, but in an air defense engagement the radar provides these necessary inputs. If your AAA radar system works, you can protect an area with far fewer guns. Because the Soviet radars were ineffective due to U.S. countermeasures, the North Koreans were forced to switch back to barrage fire tactics and bring in a large number of guns. They were too few and too late, however, to blunt the U.S. air offensive that decimated the North Koreans.

AIR POWER TAKES CENTER STAGE

General Curtis Lemay was in command of bomber forces during World War II and Korea and later became Commander of the USAF Strategic Air Command. The dismal performance of the Soviet-supplied Air Defense system during the Korean War led him to comment upon his retirement that if the U.S. had to conduct a bombing campaign against the Soviet Union during the 1950s, it would have resulted in losses no worse than normal peacetime attrition. While this statement was an exaggeration, there is no question that offensive air power held the upper hand.

Fighters were the best defense against attacking aircraft but defensive fighters had been countered in the last two wars by night flying, escort fighters, and EW. AAA was deadly but could not stop the attackers. Radar had showed promise in a supporting role during this period as well as vulnerabilities. From World War I to Korea, aircraft themselves had provided first the offense and then the defense with the upper hand in the air war. Ground-based AAA weapons had to this point only played a supporting role. This would change.

Based on the lessons of World Wars and the Korean War, the U.S and the Soviet Union raced to build large and powerful air forces. As a counter to the other side's offensive capability, new air defense weapons were also developed. The next confrontation between the superpowers would feature a new type of air defense weapon that would eventually lead to the development of Stealth technology.

2

STEALTH FIGHTER

"For those who fight for life, life has a flavor that the protected will never know."
—Steve Ritchey
Vietnam Ace

First Lieutenant Elias Danson pulled back on the stick and felt a shudder as his bomb-laden F-105 Thud rotated and clawed its way into the sky. As he reached for the gear handle, the end of the runway quickly disappeared under the nose. He was airborne on his first combat mission over North Vietnam, and one thought kept going through his mind: "please God, don't let me mess this up." Fear of dying placed a distant second in Elias Danson's thoughts—his primary fear was of making a mistake that would cause him to look bad to the other fighter pilots in the squadron.

The big fighter-bomber gained altitude and airspeed slowly as Danson turned away from Korat Air Base, in Thailand, and toward the other three jets in the flight. The Thuds were already two miles ahead of him and joining up into close formation.

Lt. Danson kept the throttle in afterburner to gain some "smash" (overtaking airspeed) and catch the flight. The airspeed gradually built up and as it hit 450 knots he eased the throttle back out of afterburner and closed the range. When he was within one mile of the flight, he opened the speedbrakes to slow down and was thrown forward against the straps of his parachute harness as the big jet decelerated. Lt. Danson breathed a sigh of relief as he slid into position beside the other F-105s. There was something reassuring about being in formation with the other jets, and the butterflies in his stomach faded away. Lt. Danson was now part of Olds 11 flight, four F-105s carrying 24,000 pounds of bombs toward the most heavily defended airspace on the planet: the Hanoi-Haiphong area of the country of North Vietnam.

In route to the target, Olds joined up with a KC-135 tanker for an in-flight refueling. Already on the tanker when Olds arrived was another flight of Thuds and four F-4s that had just topped off with fuel and were departing the tanker. They were heading to North Vietnam ahead of the Thuds to keep the North Vietnamese MiGs from bouncing the F-105s and disrupting their attack.

The other Thud flight cycled through the tanker and departed for North Vietnam. Lt. Danson pulled up on the tanker's wing with the rest of the flight as his leader slid into position behind the modified Boeing 707 tanker. The boom operator quickly stuck the refueling boom into the lead aircraft and pumped in 2,000 pounds of gas. The rest of the flight took their turn in the refueling position and within 10 minutes the flight was topped off and ready go. Lt. Danson noticed that the butterflies in his stomach were staging a comeback as Olds dropped off the tanker and left Thailand for a short flight across Laos into North Vietnam.

When clear of the tanker, the flight lead switched Olds over to the strike frequency. In the few minutes that it took to cross Laos, the world changed abruptly for Elias Danson and the rest of Olds flight. As they approached North Vietnam, their radios came alive with a crescendo of excited calls of Surface-to-Air Missile (SAM) launches as the Olds flight nervously listened in on fighting between the Wild Weasels and the North Vietnamese SA-2 sites. The Wild Weasels were specialized two-seat F-105s that were sent out ahead of the strike aircraft to find and suppress SAM sites. Lt. Danson ignored all the confused chatter on the radios and tried to concentrate and listen for the voice of his leader and his flight's call sign.

The Olds lead called for the flight to move into pod formation and turn on their jamming pods, and Lt. Danson quickly complied. The Thuds were now flying within 200 feet of each other in a close formation designed to mask their approach to enemy SAMs. Four aircraft with jamming pods, flying together in close formation, could keep the SA-2 sites from finding them. At least that was the theory. The problem with this tactic is that it relied exclusively on the jamming pod, and if that didn't work properly or the enemy had developed a counter, you were apt to find yourself flying a flaming pile of wreckage. In addition to that, it was a lousy formation for looking for MiGs because the aircraft were flying too close together to check each other's six o'clock.

All these factors were in the back of Lt. Danson's mind as he twisted himself around in the cockpit and strained to check the airspace behind his jet for MiGs. As he looked behind him, his F-105 strayed away from the flight. He was quickly made aware of this mistake by a sharp call from his leader to get back in position. As he rolled the jet up and pulled back in close to the flight an unmistakable sound crackled in his earphone. It was the sound emanating from his *Radar Homing And Warning* (RHAW) gear.

The RHAW gear, pronounced "raw," was telling him that a SA-2 SAM had found the flight. Lt. Danson glanced briefly at his RHAW scope but kept most of his attention focused on keeping up with the flight; he wasn't about to get another reprimand from his leader to stay in formation. If the pod worked correctly and if the flight stayed in position, the SAM would have trouble engaging Olds flight. These were two pretty big ifs to bet your life on, but the air war over North Vietnam was the ultimate high-stakes game, and Lt. Danson was a fighter pilot and a gambling man. He had no choice.

His mind started to drift back to his uncle's little shoe store, and how he should have taken that job he was offered. He could be showing some nice young lady something in a size 6 pump rather than having his rear end strapped to this 40,000 pound beast with every man, woman, and child in North Vietnam trying to kill him.

Suddenly, he was jolted back to reality as the Thuds made a turn toward the target and accelerated. The RHAW gear abruptly changed from a periodic chirp to the loud blare of a SAM launch warning. A SAM was in the air. Olds flight was now only five miles from the target. Lt. Danson saw the SAM, a large white telephone pole with a long plume of red flame on the end, arcing upward toward the flight. Fear gripped him along with an overpowering urge to break out of formation and dive toward the ground. He fought the urge because he knew that for a fighter pilot it is better to die than to look bad—he stayed glued in formation. The SAM rapidly closed the range and as it got closer it started to veer off course and away from Olds flight. Before he could relax, though, the flight started a violent turn and dive, and Lt. Danson jammed the throttle forward to stay in formation.

Olds was over the target and was making its dive bomb attack. As the flight dived lower toward the target, the sky filled with the deadly black puffs of AAA bursts. He watched his leader for bomb release, and when he saw the bombs come off the lead jet, he released his own. The jet bucked upward as 6,000 pounds of bombs came off the aircraft.

Now much lighter and more maneuverable, Olds flight started an erratic jink-out maneuver to spoil the aim of the AAA gunners. Lt. Danson clung to the flight as the four Thuds climbed through the AAA bursts and away from the target. The radios where full of confused calls, as SAMs crisscrossed the sky and Thuds and Phantoms filled the air over the target area. Olds flight sped through the melee in tight formation with the RHAW scope screaming out missile launch warnings. Within minutes the flight was at 15,000 feet and out of North Vietnam. A sudden calm enveloped the flight and relief swept over Lt. Elias Danson. He had survived his first trip "down town."

This was aerial warfare in the modern age: violent, high-intensity air battles, dominated by sophisticated enemy defenses and equally complex fighter countermeasures.

A NEW ERA FOR AIR DEFENSE

Offensive air power had proved decisive in World War II and Korea. In these wars the air defense consisted of fighters and AAA guns with the fighter being the most effective defensive weapon. When the offensive side used fighters of their own to gain air superiority, air defenses were ineffective. New ground-based weapons were needed to counter the offensive use of air power.

The war in Vietnam served as a testing ground for the introduction of a whole new type of revolutionary air defense weapon, the Surface-to-Air missile. After World War II, the allies captured German missile technology, and both the U.S. and the Soviets raced to build ground-based missiles that could shoot down aircraft.

The first Soviet missile developed with captured German technology was the SA-1. (The "SA-1" is the NATO designation of the missile). The SA-1 was a crude missile with limited capability but it was soon followed by the SA-2. The SA-2, shown in Figure 2-1, was introduced in Vietnam in 1965, marking the first widespread use of a SAM in combat. The SA-2, like the SA-1, was also designed to shoot down enemy bombers but it had sufficient maneuverability to also engage fighters. Advances in radar technology had made the SA-2 possible, and this missile ushered in the

Figure 2-1. SA-2 missile

modern era of air combat. In this new era, attacking aircraft would have to contend with radar-directed SAMs, fighters, and AAA.

Surface-to-Air Missiles

The SA-2 was slowly introduced around Hanoi and Haiphong by the North Vietnamese in 1965. Reconnaissance flights detected the construction of SA-2 sights in the spring of that year but U.S. fighters were forbidden to attack them. (Washington was trying to avoid escalating the war.) The air war in North Vietnam went on oblivious to this activity, and finally in July an SA-2 site became operational and fired several SAMs at F-4Cs that were bombing a munitions plant north of Hanoi. One F-4 was shot down and three others were damaged. By October of 1965, there were up to 12 North Vietnamese SAM batteries defending key targets; fighters such as the F-105 were ill-equipped to cope with this new threat. The F-105 is shown in Figure 2-2.

The U.S. attempted to counter the SAM threat with the introduction of the EB-66 jamming aircraft and direct bombing of the SA-2 sites. The EB-66 could detect a launch of a SAM, warn the attacking aircraft, and also jam the sight, which reduced the effectiveness of the SA-2. These aircraft broadcast warnings that SA-2 missiles were being launched. In addition, they provided limited jamming against the sites. At this time, strike aircraft were not equipped with RHAW gear of their own, so any warning was better than none at all.

The most effective countermeasure used against the SA-2 were called *Iron Hand missions*. These missions used specialized F-100 aircraft called Wild Weasels to seek out and mark the SA-2 sites while F-105s came in and destroyed them. This flight of F-100s and F-105s was called a hunter-killer team and the lessons they learned were bought with blood in a deadly game of cat and mouse with the SA-2. The early results were not promising as the U.S. struggled to cope with the SAMs. By December of 1965, eight Iron Hand aircraft had been shot down with only eight sites destroyed. Further improvements were made throughout the next year and a crash development program soon gave fighter aircraft an early version of RHAW gear that warned them of a missile launch.

Figure 2-2. F-105

In addition to on-board RHAW, fighter pilots were learning how to defeat the SA-2 missile in-flight. This was accomplished through a SAM break maneuver, where the fighters would dive for the ground and accelerate as soon as they saw a SAM guiding on them. They would then wait for the missile to start down on them. When they could detect details such as the fins of the missile, they started a high G pull up into the SAM. With this maneuver a fighter could cause the missile to miss by a wide enough margin to be harmless. On-board RHAW, Iron Hand missions, and new maneuvering tactics to defeat the missile in-flight caused the effectiveness of the SA-2 to drop steadily from a high of twenty percent in the first few months after it was introduced to about three percent by the spring of 1966.

Shrikes and Pods

In March of 1966 a new weapon appeared in Vietnam. It was introduced by U.S. forces, and it was called the AGM-45 Shrike. The *Shrike* was the first anti-radiation missile, or ARM, used in combat. The Shrike had a receiver that picked up the transmissions of the SA-2 target tracking radar, and then used this radar energy as a guidance beacon.

After detecting the presence of an SA-2 on their sensitive RHAW scopes the Wild Weasels (now flying F-105s) would time the shot of the Shrike to suppress the SAM site while the bombing aircraft were in the area. When the Shrike was fired, the SA-2 radar operator had the option of continuing to transmit and thereby getting his radar and possibly himself shredded by the Shrike or to shut off the radar to make the Shrike miss the target. Once the radar was turned off, the Shrike's seeker lost the target, causing the missile to go stupid. Of course with the radar off, the SAM site was blind and out of the fight until radar was turned back on.

The Shrike's introduction caused a continued decline in SA-2 effectiveness which dropped to less than two percent by the end of 1967. The Shrike had its limitations, however, such as a slow flight time and no memory of the target once SA-2 radar power was shut down. These limitations kept it from being the perfect solution to the SA-2 problem, but the Wild Weasel aircraft armed with improved RHAW and the AGM-45 Shrike put the SA-2 batteries on the defensive from 1966 to the bombing halt of 1968.

The U.S. also introduced self-protection jamming pods on fighters in late 1966 but they were plagued with problems. Dependable pods saw widespread use in the early months of 1967, and Lt. Danson's story at the beginning of this chapter describes how they were used. Aircraft flew in close formations of four aircraft with the jamming pod turned on. This destroyed the tracking solution of the SA-2 when the flight was inside the SAM's maximum range envelope of 25 miles.

The SA-2 of course could transmit more radar power than a fighter's jamming pod, so at close ranges the SA-2 could "burn through" the jamming and fire on the flight. For this reason, Weasel support remained an important part of the tactical plan, even after the introduction of an effective jamming pod. When an attacking flight planned to go inside of burn-through range on an SA-2, the Wild Weasels would be there to hose the SAM site down with Shrikes (at least that was how it was planned).

AAA Comes of Age

The air defenses of North Vietnam eventually grew to 200 prepared SA-2 sites with 20 to 30 of them active. Each active site had six launchers and a guidance radar, which the North Vietnamese moved around between the 200 prepared sites. In this way they tried to keep U.S. forces guessing about their location. Even with these large numbers, the SA-2 never regained the effectiveness that it displayed in the first few months after it was introduced.

The SA-2 was just one segment of the air defenses of North Vietnam. The most numerous and deadly air defense weapon of the war was the AAA gun. The North Vietnamese fielded over 7,000 of these guns during the war and they accounted for over 1,000 U.S. aircraft destroyed—compared with approximately 200 SA-2 kills. The AAA guns that were used ranged from 12.7-mm up to 100-mm guns with the medium calibre 37-mm and 57-mm being the most numerous. The North Vietnamese used both aimed fire and barrage fire with improved gun-laying radars. AAA owed much of its success to the presence of the SA-2, which forced attack aircraft to fly lower into the heart of the AAA engagement envelope. AAA is less effective as the altitude and airspeed of the target increases. If a fighter pilot was doing a SAM break like the one I described earlier, he got lower and slower, which made him vulnerable to the omnipresent AAA guns of the North Vietnamese forces.

Bad News for Uncle Ho

By the time the bombing of North Vietnam halted in 1968, the Soviets had installed and tested the first Integrated Air Defense System (IADS) that included SAMs, AAA, and air defense fighters. The Vietnamese used fighters selectively, and eventually shot down 80 U.S. warplanes but lost over 190 of their own.

The North Vietnamese MiG fighters did not make a significant contribution to air defense as far as numbers are concerned, but because of their presence, valuable U.S. resources were used to counter them. The presence of all three of these air defense assets working in concert posed a formidable tactical problem for the attacking forces. The U.S. technology and the valor of the pilots flying into North Vietnam stayed well ahead of the air defense improvements, and the final loss rate to the air defenses of North Vietnam was no more than two to three percent.

U.S. air power in North Vietnam was used selectively with the goal of achieving political rather than military objectives. Every war has rules of engagement, but the air war in Vietnam was fought in a web of complex changing rules that crippled the application of air power. At times during the war, for example, SAM sites could not be bombed until they became operational.

There were dozens of equally ludicrous rules in this war that cost many lives and gave confidence to an enemy with backward and inferior defenses. General Patton said there is only one tactical principle that is not subject to change. It is "To use the means at hand to inflict the maximum amount of wounds, death, and destruction on the enemy in the minimum time."

Finally, in December of 1972, General Patton's tactical principle was put into practice, and U.S. air power was unleashed on the enemy. In response to the walkout of the North Vietnamese from the Paris peace talks, U.S. forces implemented an operation called Linebacker II. This operation sent U.S. B-52 bombers, like the one shown in Figure 2-3, into the industrial heart of North Vietnam for the first time. Linebacker II was not an all-out terror campaign against the North Vietnamese as was widely reported in the press. It was instead a coordinated air attack with military objectives using heavy bombers and fighters in the same manner that they were used in North Korea. It lasted for 11 days. Of the 7,000 SAMs fired from 1964-1972, 1,000 of them where fired in this 11-day period with an effectiveness against the B-52 of only two percent. After a week the North Vietnamese had run completely out of SAMs, leaving only the AAA guns to defend the targets. By the end of the bombing the enemy was virtually defenseless, leaving the U.S. in complete control of the skies over the industrial heartland of North Vietnam (similar to the conditions in the Korean War).

Figure 2-3.   B-52 bomber

The North Vietnamese quickly responded to earlier U.S. peace initiatives and the "peace" talks in Paris resumed. In Henry Kissinger's book *The White House Years,* he quotes Bill Sullivan, who was a key negotiator at these talks. In a report to Kissinger Sullivan wrote, "(the North Vietnamese) delegation did not, repeat not comport itself like a victorious outfit which had just 'defeated the U.S. Strategic Air Force.'" He went on to describe the change in the Hanoi delegation that came about as a result of the full application of U.S. air power. This power, of course, could have been used at any time during the previous eight years of the war with the same result. A "peace" treaty followed within weeks, and the Vietnam air war came to a close for U.S. forces.

RADAR'S DOMINANT ROLE

The Vietnam War ushered in the age of the Surface-to-Air Missile and with it another change in air combat. Air forces had to contend with this threat, which added a new dimension to the air defense and intensified the race between the attackers and defenders. The Soviets poured vast resources into the development of a radar-based Integrated Air Defense System (IADS) that combined air defense fighters, AAA, and SAMs. By the time the Vietnam War ended, the Soviets had developed and fielded the SA-1,2,3,4,5,6, and 7. The North Vietnamese had only been given the SA-2. The SA-1,2,3,4,5, and 6 were all radar-guided missiles while the SA-7 was a man-portable shoulder-launched infrared guided SAM. These new SAMs were big improvements over the SA-2, and the U.S. raced to find technical and tactical solutions to overcome them.

New Tactics and Countermeasures

Countering these new weapons meant countering radar. The radar systems that populated the battlefields of the 1970s were initially neutralized by flying at very low altitudes. Radar has several problems "seeing" aircraft at altitudes below 500 feet, and attacking aircraft exploited this weakness successfully.

The first problem encountered by a radar searching for low altitude targets is clutter. When a radar beam hits the ground and is reflected back to the transmitting radar, the ground return presents a very large target. If an aircraft is flying low enough, it can be masked in this large return. Another problem is line of sight. In most cases, for a radar to "see" a target it must have a direct, uninterrupted line between the transmitting radar and the target. If there is a hill between the aircraft and the radar, the aircraft is undetectable. Curvature of the earth presents another line-of-sight problem for radar. If an aircraft is flying low, a radar cannot detect it at great distances because of the curvature of the earth. Figure 2-4 shows how this works.

The first simple aircraft counter to the widespread use of capable air defense radars was simply to underfly the radar coverage. This defeated most SAMs and fighter radars but put the aircraft in range of small arms and AAA. Since the new SAMs and fighters were more lethal than the AAA guns, this proved to be an acceptable trade-off.

In addition to flying low, attacking aircraft continued to benefit from improved on-board jamming pods and the rediscovery of chaff. Chaff was used in Vietnam by aircraft carrying special pods that dispensed high volumes of chaff and created corridors in the sky to mask attacking aircraft. This tactic proved effective but use of chaff dispensers on individual fighters did not occur until after the war. Armed with jamming pods and

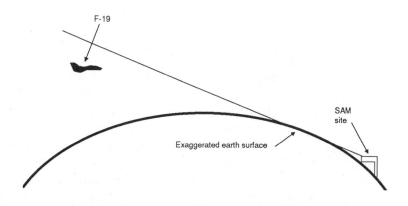

Figure 2-4.   Curvature of earth affecting line of sight

chaff dispensers, and flying at low altitudes, attack aircraft in theory could negate the radar-dependent air defenses.

Yom Kippur

The Soviet Union had observed U.S. countermeasures and tactics during and after the Vietnam war. These observations helped the Soviets develop new air defense weapons and tactics that they introduced in the Yom Kippur War.

On 6 October 1973, the Egyptians and Syrians began a surprise attack on Israel. The Arab armies initially gained ground, and the Israeli Air Force rushed into combat to stop them. The Israeli fighters came in below 200 feet to negate the SAMs but found that the newly deployed SA-6 could not be defeated by low altitude flying alone. They took very heavy losses to the SA-6 in the first few days of the war, much the same way that U.S. forces had when they first encountered the SA-2. There were reports of Israeli F-4s being hit by the SA-6 when flying below 100 feet. To solve this problem, the Israelis, with help from the U.S., developed new jamming countermeasures that helped degrade the effectiveness of the SA-6.

In addition to the SA-6, the Arabs introduced a deadly, mobile AAA gun called the ZSU-23-4. This gun had four 23-mm guns, an acquisition and tracking radar, and was mounted on a modified PT-76 tank chassis. This gun had a range of 10,000 feet and was a very deadly adversary. To make matters even worse, the Arabs introduced another Soviet weapon that was seen briefly in Vietnam—the man-portable SA-7. This IR-guided SAM was fired by the thousands with marginal results but it did point to the future direction of air defense. It had limited capability against fast-moving targets but improved versions would put all low-flying aircraft at high risk. An SA-7 SAM site could exist anywhere a man could go.

All of these new air defense weapons were countered in the Yom Kippur War by jamming and suppression by both the Israeli Army and Air Force, and the final combined effectiveness of the Arab defenses was only two to three percent. Still, the SA-6 and ZSU-23-4 had surprised the Israelis and scattered a lot of aircraft parts all over the battlefield.

This war was important because it gave the United States a clear picture of the direction of Soviet Integrated Air Defenses. The following tenets of the ground-based segment of the Soviet IADS emerged during the Yom Kippur War:

- *Mass*   Thousand of SAMs deployed in depth, providing overlapping coverage

- *Flexibility*   SAMs with both radar, IR, and optical capability, employing improved electronic countermeasures

- *Movement*   Mobile SAMs and AAA

Radar was the foundation of the Soviet IADS, and by 1981, the Russians had fielded over 4,300 radar SAMs in Central Europe, a large number of them the highly mobile SA-6 and the new SA-8. At this time some "experts" theorized that the manned aircraft would go the way of the buffalo in the face of these new radar-based air defenses. The history of air combat, however, is one of move and countermove. The U.S. responded to improved Soviet defenses with improved jamming pods, a new ARM, and several secret programs that have only recently been revealed.

ANTI-RADAR WEAPONS

The most obvious way to counter a radar threat is to attack the radar itself. By the early 1980s, U.S. forces had fielded a new generation of ARMs called the HARM (High-Speed Anti-Radiation Missile). These missiles overcame many of the limitations of the early Shrike missile. It was much faster, had a greater range, and could guide to the target even after the radar was shut down. Even though the introduction of this missile gave the attackers a boost in capability, HARM could only be carried by a few fighters that had limited range and endurance. To solve this problem, two highly classified programs emerged.

The first of these was code-named "Seek Spinner." Seek Spinner was a small ground-launched, anti-radiation drone. These drones were designed to seek out specific radars and attack by diving into them. If the radar shut down, they would continue to orbit over the site until it came back on. This drone had a very small warhead compared to the HARM but it was large enough to destroy a radar antenna. In combat, Seek Spinner would be launched by the hundreds and would orbit the battlefield for hours, harassing and destroying enemy radars.

Another more sophisticated ARM program was code-named "Tacit Rainbow." This missile, shown in Figure 2-5, was built using cruise missile technology. It was designed to have the flexibility to engage a wide variety of radars and have long range and endurance. Tacit Rainbow is similar to Seek Spinner but Tacit Rainbow is a larger, more capable system with a much bigger warhead. Figure 2-6 shows the results of a Tacit Rainbow missile hit on a mobile radar van. The missile in this test was not equipped with its standard 40lb warhead and still broke the chassis of the target. Both of these systems have been turned on and off due to budget cuts but Tacit Rainbow will probably be developed and give U.S. forces a powerful capability.

STEALTH TECHNOLOGY

A less obvious way to counter the radar threat was the development of Stealth technology. *Stealth technology* is a broad term that refers to the reduction of radar and IR profiles (signatures). Two formally "Black" stealth programs, the F-117 and the B-2, have recently been made public. A *Black program* is one that is kept completely hidden from view with even the existence of the program kept secret. In response to the growing radar threat, U.S. technology, aided by the use of supercomputer design and advance materials, strove to find the ultimate technical solution to the massive radar-based Soviet defense system. This expansive (and expensive) program produced the F-117 Stealth Fighter code-named Senior

Figure 2-5.   Tacit Rainbow missile

Figure 2-6.   Van destroyed by a Tacit Rainbow missile

Figure 2-7.   B-2 bomber

Trend and the B-2 bomber. The B-2 bomber is shown in Figure 2-7. Both the F-117 and the B-2 bomber feature "low-observable" or reduced radar and IR signatures.

    The move to create aircraft with a low radar and IR signature is the latest move in the thrust and counter-thrust between attacking and defending forces that began in World War I. This move toward Stealth technology, like other technological breakthroughs, will have a very profound impact on air combat, giving the attackers a substantial advantage. Air defense forces have relied on radar since World War II, and the Soviets in particular lean heavily on radar technology. Stealth technology holds the promise of rendering this massive Soviet air defense system obsolete. It also further widens the technological gap between the Third World powers and the U.S. The introduction of the hand-held IR SAM threatened to give even backward nations a formidable air defense capability. The introduction of night flying Stealth aircraft has changed the game, however, making these weapons useless. While counters to Stealth technology will eventually be developed, they will not be cheap or widely deployed. For the next decade, Stealth will give the U.S. control of the night skies over the battlefield. Sleep well, Mohammar.

The F-117 Stealth Fighter

In November of 1988, the U.S. Air Force briefed the press on a new Stealth aircraft. The Air Force has taken the F-117 out of the black world, and a few details are now emerging. Figure 2-8 shows an official Air Force photograph of the F-117. The jet is currently being flown out of a secret base north of Las Vegas, Nevada. Approximately 50 of these jets have been built by Lockheed in their California plant.

The F-117 flies most of its missions at night. Its recent employment in Panama suggests it will be used to bomb high-value targets. Exact weapon load, range, and other performance characteristics have still not been released by the Air Force.

The Stealth Fighter is made primarily of aluminum with *radar absorbent material* (RAM) added to the skin of the aircraft. It acquires its radar-evading properties from this RAM material and its unique shape. The shape of the aircraft represents the mid-to-late 1970s state-of-the-art in Stealth technology. The F-117 employs highly swept wings and an angular fuselage shaped to reduce its *radar cross section* (RCS) from most angles. Reduced RCS is not possible from every angle so tactics are very important and will be covered in detail later in the book.

The aircraft weighs approximately 42,000 pounds and has a wing span of 44 feet and a length of 60 feet. It is believed to have an internal bomb bay along with a retractable IR sensing device. The aircraft undoubtedly conducts its missions in radio silence, and retractable radio antenna have been observed on the belly of the aircraft and aft of the cockpit on the top of the fuselage.

Unfortunately, fighter design is similar to other facets of life—you don't get something for nothing. One look at the F-117 tells you that this jet is not built for maneuverability or speed. To achieve its Stealth characteristics it has traded off normal fighter performance, along with cockpit visibility, for reduced RCS and IR signature. Still, the F-117 represents a great leap forward in capability for the U.S. Using the lessons learned from

Figure 2-8.   F-117 Stealth fighter

this aircraft we can go on to build even better fighters with Stealth characteristics.

STEALTH COMBAT

The F-19 simulation creates a modern tactical environment that allows the pilot to fly and fight in a Stealth aircraft. The F-19 pilot is immersed in the combat of the future where concealment and firepower are the key attributes of air warfare. The rest of the book will teach you how to succeed in the challenging environment of the F-19 Stealth Fighter Simulation.

3

F-19 FUNDAMENTALS

> *Discipline is based on pride in the profession of arms, meticulous attention to details, and on mutual respect and confidence. Discipline must be a habit so ingrained that it is stronger than the excitement of battle or the fear of death."*
> —General George S. Patton

You have crossed the coast of Libya and are skillfully flying your F-19 through the rugged computer-generated terrain when a MiG-29 appears on your tactical display. Quickly, you call up your sidewinders, check the optics sensor for a missile lock indication, and hose off a missile. Unfortunately this missile turns out to be a snake killer and nose dives for the desert floor. You're too close to shoot another missile so you merge with the MiG and wrap the jet around in a steep bank turn to get into gun parameters. The fight gets tighter and tighter as you think to yourself, "if

I could just get rid of that loud obnoxious noise in the cockpit, I could concentrate better on killing this sand gomer." Suddenly, the nose drops, and a piece of rock-hard mother earth rises quickly to turn your jet into scrap metal. Just before you get a face full of desert you realize your mistake—the stall horn—you stalled the jet.

I am sure you have experienced this or other very similar ways of crashing in the F-19 simulation. Flying into the ground is a very common way to end a mission. The incident just described is due to what fighter pilots call *channelized attention*—caused by being over tasked or having bad habit patterns.

This chapter will cover setting up the missions and the F-19 flying fundamentals. With this knowledge you can build flying discipline and habit patterns that will keep you alive in the simulation. A fighter pilot builds these habits early in his flying career and uses them as a foundation to build more advanced air combat techniques. As an F-19 pilot *you* also must develop good habit patterns and flight discipline or you will never achieve your maximum potential. Understanding the basics allows you to execute them as second nature. Once basic flying skills are second nature you will have more grey matter freed up to perfect your fighting skills. The road to learning flight fundamentals is a rocky one for the F-19 pilot or the real fighter pilot.

An incident involving a friend of mine is a real-world example of what channelized attention can do. This story also illustrates just how uneven and hazardous the road to becoming a fighter pilot can be. This friend, who will remain nameless due to his size and disposition, landed a T-37 "gear up" when he was a student in pilot training. When asked why he didn't go around or put his gear down when the instructor out at the end of the runway told him to over the radio, he replied, "I couldn't hear the radio because the 'gear up' warning horn was too loud."

This response, though an accurate assessment of his feeble mental state at the time, did nothing to calm his flight commander, whose personality bordered on hysteria even under normal circumstances. The resulting reprimand my buddy received is now a part of the folklore of Undergraduate Pilot Training. So take heart when you bite the dust in the F-19 simulation. We all have to go through frustrating experiences to learn fighter flying skills. Hopefully yours won't be as bad as the one that my friend went through. The only way to get better in the jet is through academic knowledge and practice. This chapter will give you the necessary academic tools.

AERODYNAMICS

Most fighter pilots know the same amount about the aeronautical principles that govern their jets as they do about romance—just enough to be confused. There is really not a lot you need to know about aerodynamics, which is fortunate because teaching a fighter pilot anything other than very basic aerodynamics is like teaching a pig to sing. It is a waste of time, and it angers the pig.

The Forces on the Jet

The F-19 pilot should know the basic forces that act on an aircraft in flight. Figure 3-1 depicts these forces and their direction in relation to the F-19.

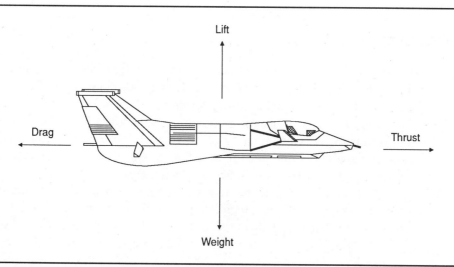

Figure 3-1.   Forces acting on the jet

Thrust is created by the engines and pushes the jet forward through the sky. Throttle settings control thrust. As you push the throttle up, you convert jet fuel into noise and produce more thrust (and speed). The one thing to keep in mind though is that the higher the thrust you command, the more fuel you burn.

Lift is the force that counters the weight of the aircraft and enables it to fly. Lift is produced by the aircraft wings, and is directed perpendicular to your flight path, straight out the top of the jet. This force is the *lift vector*.

Drag acts opposite thrust and is created two ways. The first way is by basic aerodynamic shape. Pushing anything through air causes friction between the air and the aircraft, which is known as *form drag* or *parasite drag*. You can reduce this type of drag by having a smooth, aerodynamic shape. A bullet has a very *clean* aerodynamic shape and low parasite drag, for example, while a brick has a *dirty* high-drag shape. The other type of drag is called *induced drag*. Induced drag is caused by the lift being generated by the wings. I will not go into why this occurs because it starts to border on pig singing lessons. Just remember that as you turn the aircraft tightly you are commanding more lift from the wings and thus more induced drag.

Weight is the last force acting on the jet, and it pulls the aircraft toward the earth.

Maneuvering the Jet

Building on your newly acquired in-depth knowledge of aerodynamics, let's discuss aircraft maneuvering from a fighter pilot's perspective. There are only three things you can do with a jet: *roll, turn,* and *accelerate/decelerate.* Rolling is the act of positioning the wings (and thus your lift vector). As you sit in your "cockpit," imagine a line that runs from the nose of the jet through the aircraft and out the tail. This line is called the *roll axis,* and roll is movement of the aircraft wings around this line.

Turn is movement of the nose that occurs as a result of rolling the aircraft. When you roll the wings of the aircraft and then stop the roll, you establish a *bank angle.* This angle is measured between the wings of your aircraft and the horizon. When you establish a bank, the aircraft turns in the direction of the low wing.

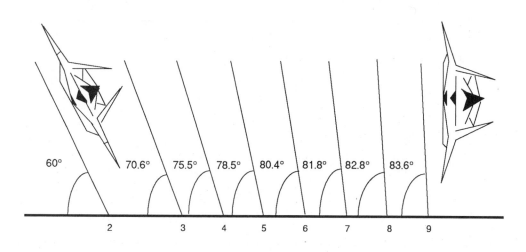

Figure 3-2.   *G*s and corresponding bank angle

The rate at which the aircraft turns is determined in part by the *G*s that the pilot pulls. The higher the *G*s, or rate of movement of the aircraft's nose, commanded by the pilot, the faster the aircraft turns (assuming a constant airspeed). During a level turn (assuming a constant altitude), there is a relationship between bank angle and *G*s. If the pilot wants to execute a 2*G* level turn, for example, he must use 60 degrees of aircraft bank. A 6*G* turn requires 80 degrees of bank. Figure 3-2 shows aircraft *G*s and the corresponding proper bank angle for a level turn. If you do not bank the aircraft at the proper bank angle for a particular *G* load, you will climb or descend. If you were at 60 degrees of bank and pulled 3*G*s, the aircraft would climb. If you only pull 1.5*G*s at 60 degrees of bank, the aircraft would descend.

Accelerating/decelerating is the change of aircraft speed because of changes in thrust, drag, or aircraft nose position in relation to the earth (weight).

In later chapters we will discuss close-in air-to-air maneuvering, which is nothing more than positioning your *lift vector* in relation to another aircraft. For now all you have to understand is the relationship of

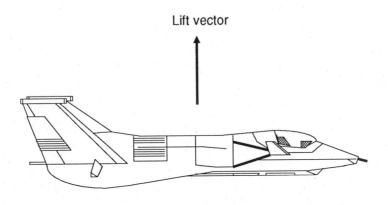

Figure 3-3. Lift vector

your lift vector position to the horizon with respect to *G*s. Figure 3-3 shows the aircraft lift vector coming straight up out of the top of the jet. This lift vector is controlled by the pilot with the control stick. When the pilot pulls back on the control stick, he commands a bigger lift vector and higher *G*. Since the aircraft moves in the direction of this vector, the more *G*s, the faster the turn.

Stalls

To understand why an aircraft *stalls*, you first need to understand *Angle of Attack* or *AOA*. AOA is the angle formed by the body of the aircraft and its flight path. In the F-19, the AOA of the jet is the difference between the Gun Cross and the Flight Path Marker. Figure 3-4 depicts AOA from both a side view and the F-19 HUD (Heads Up Display) view. The Gun Cross represents the nose of the aircraft while the Flight Path Marker shows the jet's path through the sky.

AOA is related to lift in that the greater the AOA, the greater the lift being produced by the jet. As a jet slows down it needs to produce more lift

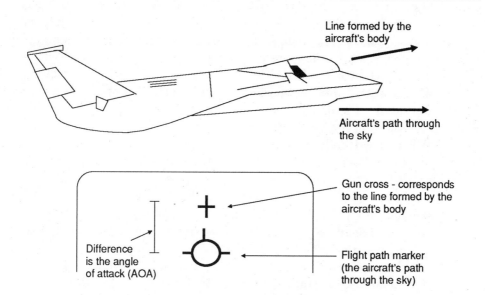

Figure 3-4. AOA from a side view and HUD view

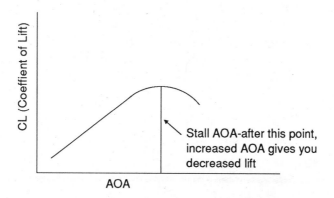

Figure 3-5. Lift-AOA/Stall curve

to stay in the air. Lift produced must be equal to weight, and AOA increases to produce this lift. Each aircraft has a specific AOA limit. When this AOA is exceeded, the lift produced goes down instead of up and a stall occurs. An aircraft stalls when its stall AOA is reached, and Figure 3-5 shows the lift/AOA curve of the F-19. The place in the curve where the graph slopes down is the stall point. Notice that lift keeps increasing with AOA until you reach the stall point.

Slowing down will eventually cause you to stall because you will have to keep jacking the nose of the jet up to produce more lift as airspeed decreases. Eventually you will get to the maximum AOA and the aircraft will stall. When a stall occurs you are no longer flying an aircraft—you are a passenger, riding an expensive pile of scrap iron toward the cold, hard ground. Once you reduce the AOA, this scrap iron will transform back into an aircraft again. If you wait too long to reduce the AOA, however, the jet will again transform into scrap metal.

When you turn the jet at high G, two related events occur that can lead to an aircraft stall. The first is that at higher G you are producing more lift and more induced drag, which causes your jet to slow down. The second is that any time you command high G, you raise the AOA and get closer to a stall. When you enter a high G turn, your AOA goes up immediately with the increase of Gs; as you slow down it goes even higher, placing you near the stall AOA. This principle is important for F-19 pilots to understand. The F-19 stalls easily during high G maneuvers, and it is critical that you know why so you can avoid a stall or react properly if one occurs. (By contrast, a high performance aircraft such as an F-16 Falcon is so powerful that it will not bleed off very much airspeed during high G maneuvering, so stalls are not a concern.)

THE BRIEFING

It's time to get serious about strapping on the F-19 and learning Stealth Fighter basics from inside the jet. A fighter mission consists of a briefing, preflight, the sortie itself, and the debrief. The briefing covers the mission

objectives and how you will accomplish them. This flight will be a basic
aircraft handling sortie.

Mission Objectives

- Review cockpit layout and simulation set-up
- Learn basic aircraft handling
- Practice take-off and landing procedures

Mission Overview

- Review set-up simulation
- Review cockpit displays and controls
- Perform take off and climb out
- Perform shallow and steep turns
- Practice stall recoveries
- Practice landings

Figure 3-6 shows the profile of our mission.

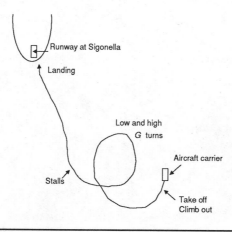

Figure 3-6.   Mission profile

PREFLIGHT

F-19 has menu driven introduction and "set up" pages. Before we take off and fly the mission, we will go through some of these pages as part of our preflight preparation. The first screens to come up in F-19 are used to "set up" control of the jet in the simulation.

The first page asks you if you have a joystick connected. If you do, it takes you through a calibration routine. After calibrating the joystick, the next screen allows you to select a number that corresponds to your monitor type (VGA, EGA, and so on). After accomplishing these easy steps you enter the simulation itself.

The first screen up is the F-19 screen. This screen is shown in Figure 3-7, and it is accompanied by a snappy little tune. This tune is not bad the first 200 to 300 times you hear it but after that you may want to stop the music. To do this and move on to the next screen, hit any key on the keyboard.

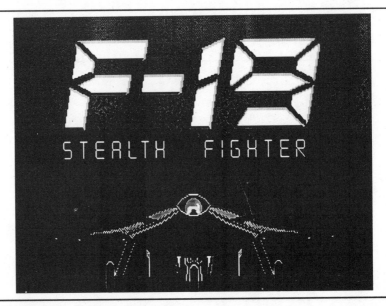

Figure 3-7. F-19 opening screen

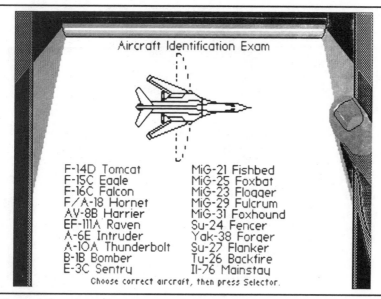

Figure 3-8.   Aircraft identification exam

Aircraft Identification Exam

Figure 3-8 shows the aircraft identification exam. This provides the F-19 pilot a platform view of a combat aircraft at the top of the screen. The rest of the screen lists the aircraft that the pilot can choose from to match the aircraft shape at the top of the page. To move among the choices, use your joystick or the arrow keys (↑, ↓, →, ←) on the keyboard. After selecting your answer, use the ENTER key to input it. The program will let you know if you made the correct choice by flashing a message at the bottom of the screen.

Duty Roster

The Duty Roster page is shown in Figure 3-9. This page has a list of pilots and their status. Pilots are either active, killed in action (KIA), or retired. Only active pilots can be selected.

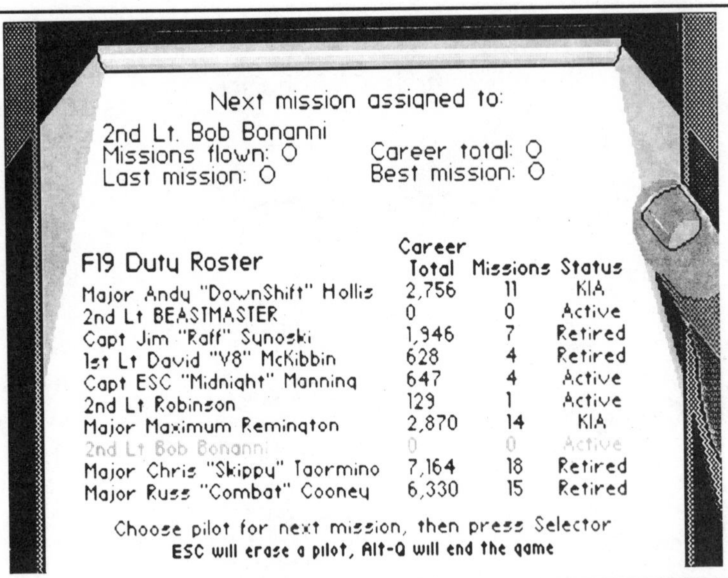

Next mission assigned to:

2nd Lt. Bob Bonanni
Missions flown: O   Career total: O
Last mission: O   Best mission: O

F19 Duty Roster	Career Total	Missions	Status
Major Andy "DownShift" Hollis	2,756	11	KIA
2nd Lt BEASTMASTER	0	0	Active
Capt Jim "Raff" Synoski	1,946	7	Retired
1st Lt David "V8" McKibbin	628	4	Retired
Capt ESC "Midnight" Manning	647	4	Active
2nd Lt Robinson	129	1	Active
Major Maximum Remington	2,870	14	KIA
2nd Lt Bob Bonanni	0	0	Active
Major Chris "Skippy" Taormino	7,164	18	Retired
Major Russ "Combat" Cooney	6,330	15	Retired

Choose pilot for next mission, then press Selector
ESC will erase a pilot, Alt-Q will end the game

Figure 3-9.   Duty Roster page

To select a pilot, use the joystick or up and down arrow keys (↑, ↓) to highlight a pilot's name. His total score will be listed beside his name along with his number of missions and his status. When you highlight a pilot's name, a more detailed record will appear at the top of the page. This record will tell you the number of points that he scored on his best mission and his last mission. In addition, it will show you the number and types of medals he has earned. To enter the game as a particular pilot, highlight the name you want, and hit ENTER. If you wish to fly under a new name, highlight the pilot name you've been using, and press the ESC key. This will erase the pilot's name and let you type in a new one. Now hit ENTER to go on to the next page.

Mission Assignment Page

This page is shown in Figure 3-10 and is used to set up the F-19 missions. When you first enter the Mission Assignment page, you get preselected mission variables on the right-top corner of the screen. The left corner of

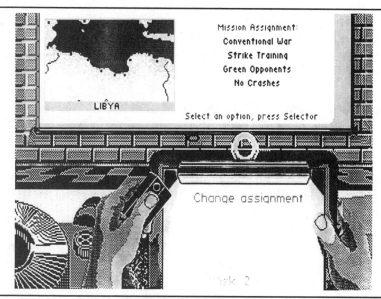

Figure 3-10.   Mission Assignment page

the screen shows a map of one of four areas of the world where the mission will take place. At the bottom of the page are two pilot selectable choices. These let you accept the mission that is outlined at the top of the page or change the mission. You move between these choices with the up and down arrow keys ($\uparrow$,$\downarrow$) and select your choice with the ENTER key.

If you accept the mission, the mission variables at the top of the page will be inserted into the computer and a mission will emerge on the next page. If you elect to change the mission, you select the "Change Mission" option, which allows you to stay on the Mission Assignment Page and select new mission variables.

The bottom-right corner of the page will move the pilot through a menu of mission variables. The following list gives you the choices:

Mission Area   Includes Libya, the Persian Gulf, North Cape, and Central Europe.

Level of Conflict   Cold War, Limited War, and Conventional War.

Mission Type   Includes Air-to-Air, Strike, Air-to-Air Training, and Strike Training.

Opponent Skill Level   Green, Regular, Veteran, Elite.

Landing Realism   No Crash, Easy Landings, and Realistic Landings.

After selecting Landing Realism, the Intelligence Briefing page will appear. For today's training mission select Change Mission, and then select Libya, Conventional War, Strike Training, Regular Opponents, and Easy Landings. By selecting Libya for a training mission, you will always get the same departure and recovery location as well as the same targets and mission profile. This is not true when selecting training missions for the other scenarios (North Cape, Central Europe, the Persian Gulf).

Our training mission will not involve fighting so I will cover some of these variables later in the book.

When selecting the degree of realism for landings, note the parameters changing in the top-right corner of the screen as you step through the different options. The Easy Landing option lets you touch down at 800 feet per second (1600 feet per second on a carrier). If you select Realistic Landings these values drop to 400 for runways and 800 for carriers. Landings are a very critical and difficult part of the game, so we will discuss F-19 landing techniques at great length later in this chapter.

Intelligence Briefing Page

The Intelligence Briefing page is shown in Figure 3-11. This page gives the pilot detailed tactical information to plan his mission. Included on this page is a large map of the area. On this mission, note that we are starting from an aircraft carrier in the Mediterranean Sea. We will go over this page in detail when we discuss tactics later in the book, so for now, page down to the last choice on the menu at the far right side of the page using the down arrow key (↓). Once you get to the Exit Briefing Room option, press ENTER.

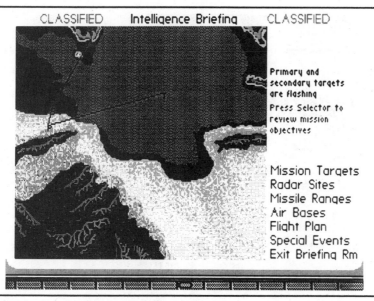

CLASSIFIED   Intelligence Briefing   CLASSIFIED

Primary and
secondary targets
are flashing
Press Selector to
review mission
objectives

Mission Targets
Radar Sites
Missile Ranges
Air Bases
Flight Plan
Special Events
Exit Briefing Rm

Figure 3-11.   Intelligence Briefing page

Armament Page

The Armament Page, shown in Figure 3-12, tells you what weapons are loaded in your jet and gives you the option to change them. You move between the different options with the joystick or arrow keys ($\uparrow$, $\downarrow$, $\rightarrow$, $\leftarrow$). Each time you highlight a new option, the capabilities of the weapon appear in the upper-left corner of the page. You can move around the weapons list looking at the different options. When you find one that you wish to load, hit the ENTER key and watch for one of the four different bomb bay areas to flash. If you hit the ENTER key again, you will replace the weapons in the flashing bay with what you just selected. If you want to place the newly selected weapons in a different position, you can use the joystick or arrows ($\uparrow$, $\downarrow$, $\rightarrow$, $\leftarrow$) to highlight a different weapons bay. When you get to the desired one, press the ENTER key. When you're finished arming the jet go

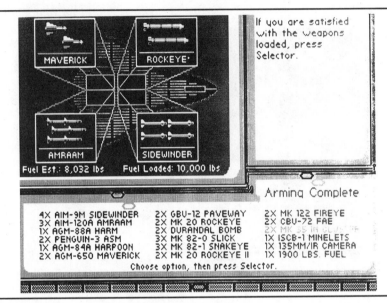

Figure 3-12. Armament page

to the Arming Complete option and press the ENTER key. Again, we will not be fighting on this mission so just go to Arming Complete and press ENTER.

Final Choice Page

The Final Choice, shown in Figure 3-13, lets the pilot go back and make changes or execute the mission. You move between the options in the same way that you did in the previous pages—via the joystick or up and down arrows (↑, ↓). To execute the desired option use the ENTER key. We are finally ready to mount this beast. Hit the Begin Mission option.

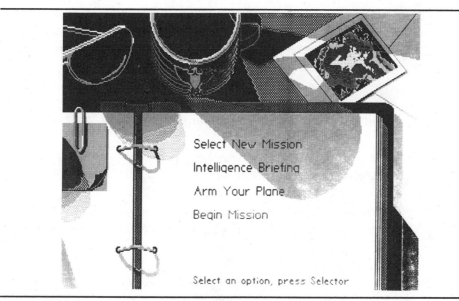

Figure 3-13.   Final Choice page

THE COCKPIT

You are now in the seat of power, the F-19 cockpit. The F-19 cockpit presents the new pilot with a dazzling array of displays and controls. Before we describe these in detail, let's take a look around. There are two primary viewing perspectives in F-19. These are views out of the cockpit and views out of the aircraft. The following list tells you what you are actually seeing in these views and how to call them up.

Out of the Aircraft Views

Slot View   Press SHIFT-F1. This view looks directly behind and slightly low of the F-19. It's only slightly interesting and not very useful.

Chase Plane View   Press SHIFT-F2. This view is from a short distance behind your plane. I have used this view at times when flying acrobatics. It gives you a perspective of where you are in relation to the horizon when you go over the top.

Side View   Press SHIFT-F3. This view is the best one for checking that your landing gear are down prior to landing.

Missile View   Press SHIFT-F4. This view allows the pilot to ride a missile that is launched by the F-19. It is an excellent way to enjoy a missile kill.

Tactical View   Press SHIFT-F5. This view allows you to see from the F-19 to the target. It can be used in air-to-air combat to see the geometry of the fight.

Inverse Tactical View   Press SHIFT-F6. This view allows the pilot to see his jet from the enemy's perspective. This is a very good way to critique your air-to-air defense reactions and your air-to-ground attacks.

In all of these views except the Chase Plane View, the pilot can magnify the view or make it smaller. Hitting **Z** will zoom the picture while hitting **X** will unzoom the view. In addition, the viewing angle of all these screens can be changed to any angle between 60 and 120 degrees by pressing the **C** key.

Out of the Cockpit Views

View Ahead   Press SHIFT-/. This view is used to look out the front of the jet (not through the HUD).

View Rear   Press SHIFT-. (period). This provides the pilot with a six o'clock view.

View Left   Press SHIFT-, (comma). This view is out the left side of the jet.

View Right   Press SHIFT-M. This view is out the right side of the aircraft.

In both out of the cockpit and out of the aircraft views, you can always return to the inside the cockpit (HUD) view by pressing the F1 key.

There are probably as many ways to use these views as there are F-19 pilots. Go through some of them as you sit on the deck of the carrier waiting to take off. I personally don't use them very much because I find it disconcerting to be "out of the cockpit" or not looking at the HUD, but I'm sure there are plenty of pilots out there who take advantage of them.

The HUD (Heads Up Display)

The Heads Up Display is the primary cockpit display. It is used to control and fly the aircraft as well as point and shoot the weapons. Figure 3-14 shows the F-19 fighter HUD with the important displays marked. The HUD in this picture is in the NAV (Navigation) mode. The HUD has two other modes—Air-to-Air mode and Air-to-Ground mode. You move be-

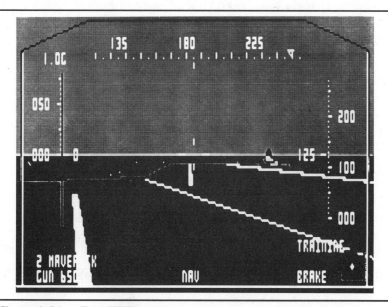

Figure 3-14.   F-19 HUD

tween them with the F2 key. The following list explains the functions of the non-weapons displays of the HUD.

Flight Path Marker   The Flight Path Marker is a circle with small wings and a tail. It shows the pilot the path of the aircraft through the sky. In the F-19 simulation, if you place the Flight Path Marker on the horizon you will not climb or descend. If you place the Flight Path Marker in a position where the horizon becomes invisible (like in a steep dive or climb), then Pitch Bars appear in 10 degree increments. These bars give the pilot a pitch and bank reference when the horizon is out of view.

Gun Cross   The Gun Cross is also called the nose indicator in the F-19 simulation. This reference is fixed on the HUD and is second in importance only to the Flight Path Marker as a reference. It shows the pilot where the nose of the aircraft (and the gun) is pointing. In a later chapter, I will show how to use this reference to win fame and fortune.

Airspeed Scale   The Airspeed Scale on the left side of the HUD consists of a moving scale and a fixed line in the middle marking the airspeed. An exact digital reading of F-19 airspeed is presented to the right of this fixed mark.

Altitude Scale   This scale is presented the same way as the Airspeed Scale except on the right side of the HUD. A moving scale shows aircraft altitude with the exact altitude presented to the left of the fixed mark in the center of the scale. When the jet gets above 1,000 feet, the scale changes to thousands. For example, 2,000 is presented as 2K.

Heading Scale   The Heading Scale is presented at the top of the HUD with 000 being North, 090 being East, and so on. There is a stationary center vertical line to mark the heading.

INS Steer Point Indicator   This indicator shows the heading the aircraft must fly to get to the selected waypoint. It appears on the heading scale as a small diamond that remains fixed at the proper heading.

Stall Speed Indicator   This important indicator comes up from the bottom of the airspeed scale. It appears as a line that runs up the side of the indicator. When it reaches the fixed horizontal airspeed indicator mark, the aircraft stalls.

VVI Indicator   The VVI Indicator is a small line that shows F-19 *vertical velocity*. Vertical velocity is how fast the aircraft is climbing or descending. This indicator, in conjunction with the Landing VVI Cue, gives the pilot an indication of whether or not he can safely land the aircraft using the present rate of descent.

Landing VVI Cue   This cue is a small colored triangle that appears when the landing gear are down. It moves down the Altitude Scale to mark a spot that the VVI Indicator should not go below for a safe landing.

Control Stick Indicator   This indicator is a box that appears in the lower-right corner of the HUD when you are flying F-19 without a joystick. Inside the box is a small cross that marks the position of the control stick.

G Indicator   The *G* Indicator (or *G* meter) appears at the upper-left corner of the HUD and it shows current *G*s.

Mode Indicator   The words "NAV," "AIR-AIR," and "AIR-GROUND" will appear at the bottom of the HUD to indicate the selected mode.

Flight Equipment Indicator   In the lower-right corner of the HUD the words "FLAPS" appears to indicate that the flaps are down. The word "BRAKE" also appears in this same location if the aircraft speed brakes have been opened in flight or if the jet is on the ground and the wheel brakes have been applied.

The MFDs

The most prominent feature of the cockpit are the two large Multi-Functional Displays (MFDs) located in the center of each side of the cockpit.

There is a wide range of pilot selectable options that can be displayed on each MFD but for this training flight we will cover only three options.

Figure 3-15 shows the MFDs when you first climb into the cockpit for this mission. The right MFD shows the *Mission Orders screen,* which gives the pilot a rundown of the mission. By pressing F7, you can shift the right MFD to the *Waypoint screen.* This screen, shown in Figure 3-16, lists the waypoints that the computer has selected for the mission. When this screen appears in the right MFD, the left MFD shows a route map with lines connecting the waypoints. In addition, the present position of the aircraft is shown as a flashing square on the end of the line; as the F-19 makes its way along the route, the line segments disappear.

At the bottom of the Waypoint screen there is a horizontal fuel gauge that shows the gas remaining in the jet. When the level of fuel gets dangerously low, the FUEL light, which is located in between the MFDs, will illuminate.

Telelight Panel

The Telelight Panel consists of the landing GEAR light, the AUTOpilot light, and a smaller warning light panel. We will cover the warning light panel later. The AUTOpilot illuminates when the autopilot is engaged. To engage the autopilot, you hit the **7** key. The landing GEAR light comes on to signal that the gear are down and locked. To lower or raise the gear press the **6** key.

The Throttle

The throttle is on the right side of the cockpit. To push the throttle up and increase engine thrust, hit the **=** key. To decrease thrust and pull the throttle back, press the **–** key. To go to full power with one keystroke, press SHIFT-=. To retard the power to idle with one key stroke, press SHIFT- – .

The F-19 simulation has no cockpit gauge to show engine performance information; however, you can approximate how much thrust you are commanding by looking at the throttle position. A bar at the bottom of the throttle gives you a relative gauge of how much power you are commanding. When the throttle is all the way forward, it is at the top of the bar and

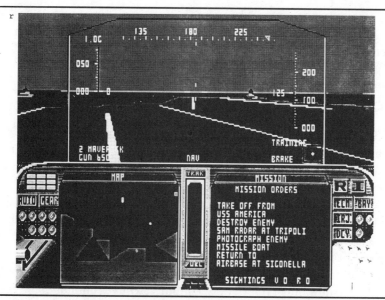

Figure 3-15.   MFD displays upon entering the cockpit

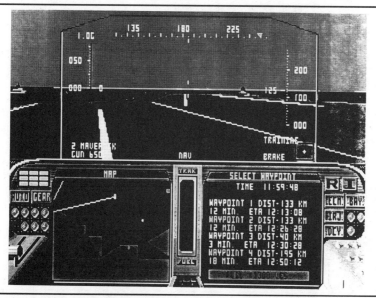

Figure 3-16.   Waypoint screen

at 100 percent power. When the throttle is all the way back, it is at the bottom of the bar and at 0 percent power. Using this system you can roughly set your power.

The Stick

All fighters, even ones as unmaneuverable as the Stealth fighter, are controlled with a stick. In F-19 you have the option of using a joystick or the keyboard to act as the control stick. Figure 3-17 shows two different keyboard layouts.

To roll the aircraft, you hit either the → or ← key. Each time you press the key, the aircraft will roll farther in that direction. To move the nose in the direction of the top of the HUD, press the ↑ key. To move the nose toward the bottom of the HUD, press the ↓ key. When you make these inputs you will notice the cross inside the Control Stick Indicator moves to show you how much relative stick input you have commanded. When using

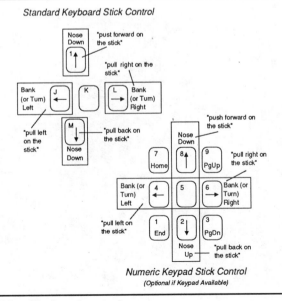

Figure 3-17. Keyboard controls

a joystick you simply move the stick in the desired direction of nose movement. When you center the joystick you remove the control input and neutralize the flight controls.

To adjust the sensitivity of the stick, press the INS key. Each time you press this key, a number from 1 to 3 will momentarily appear in the HUD, giving you a clue to the stick sensitivity. The higher the number the more sensitive the stick. What this means is that you command a large control input with a small movement of the controls. If you adjust this number upward in flight, be sure to reset the sensitivity prior to the landing pattern.

TAKEOFF

You suspected that at some point we would finally finish all that preflight information and get off the ground. The time has finally come to make some jet noise.

Notice that the jet is sitting on an aircraft carrier poised for takeoff. The first thing you should do in this position is lower the flaps by pressing the **9** key. After the flaps are down, run the engine up to full power by holding down the SHIFT key and hitting the **=** key. The engine will quickly advance to full power and produce a loud whine. In addition, the throttle will move to the full power position.

To adjust the sounds (including engine noise), hold down the ALT key and press the **V** key. This will toggle you through four sound levels. Each time you press **V**, a number corresponding to one of the following sound levels will momentarily appear at the top of the HUD:

3	all sounds
2	all sounds except engine background noise
1	firing and explosions only, no warnings
0	no sounds

Since the jet is on a carrier, the brakes are set and you are hooked to the catapult. You can run the power up but you will not move. If the jet is positioned on a runway the brake is *not* automatically set; on a runway, the aircraft will start moving as soon as you run the power up.

To release the catapult you press **0** (the brakes key). The jet will quickly accelerate down the deck and off the end of the ship. As you accelerate, the Stall Speed Indicator line will start dropping on the Airspeed Scale of the HUD. When this line is below the horizontal line on the Airspeed Scale, you can start your rotation. (I personally don't use this indicator for a takeoff cue but it's there if you need it.)

In the F-19 you can always get safely off the runway or carrier deck by rotating the aircraft between 140-150 knots. So to take off, let the aircraft accelerate to this speed range, and then rotate. Rotate by pulling smoothly back on the stick until the Flight Path Marker is above the horizon. Figure 3-18 shows the correct position of the jet just after takeoff. Check your altitude. When you see it climbing through 200 feet, raise the gear by pressing **6** and raise the flaps by pressing the **9** key.

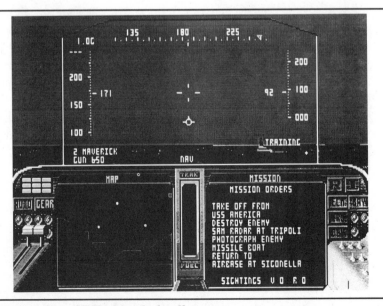

Figure 3-18.   HUD view of takeoff

Takeoffs on a runway are the same as from the carrier deck except the brakes are not automatically set. When taking off from a runway, set the brakes by hitting the **0** key. After running up the power to 100 percent, release the brakes by hitting the **0** key again. Do not take off by running the power up without the brakes engaged. If the brakes are not engaged the aircraft will slowly accelerate down the runway as you advance the power, and you'll lose valuable runway. Besides, this type of takeoff is very bad form since it is used by the trash haulers (also called targets—targets are the kind of aircraft you can stand up in, and they usually have restrooms and people onboard who serve you drinks.)

When taking off in a fighter you stand on the brakes to hold the jet in position while you push the power up. You then check your engine and release the brakes. There are several good reasons why you should follow these same tried and true fighter procedures in the F-19 simulation, but the best reason is: this is the way we do it in a fighter.

CLIMB OUT AND CRUISE

After takeoff, climb up to 2,000 feet and level off by pushing forward on the joystick or by hitting the ↑ key until the Flight Path Marker is level with the horizon. Pull the throttle back one notch by pressing the – key. Now pause the jet by holding down the ALT key and pressing the **P** key. This will freeze the simulation.

Before we continue, lets review some aircraft handling basics. Climbing and diving in the F-19 is very straightforward. To climb or dive you just push the control stick forward or aft (with the ↑ or ↓ arrow keys or the joystick). Turning is not so straightforward. I'm sure by now every F-19 pilot knows how to turn the jet. However, executing a proper turn is vital when fighting air-to-air so I will review the proper technique.

To turn the jet, you first roll to set your lift vector. The lift vector points straight out the top of the HUD. You roll the jet with the ← and → keys or by moving the joystick left or right. When the wings are set, you pull back on the stick to command *G*. This is done with the ↓ key or by pulling back on the joystick. The more you pull back, the more *G*s you produce, which gives you a greater lift vector and a faster turn. Figure 3-3 earlier in the chapter shows the bank angle required for level turns using different *G* loadings.

Low *G* Turns

Take the F-19 out of the Pause mode by hitting any key on the keyboard. Now that we are flying again, let's practice some low and high *G* turns.

To execute a low *G* turn, set the power between 80 and 100 percent, and roll the jet into a bank of approximately 60 degrees. Then pull back on the stick gently (or hit the ↓ key once or twice) until you see about 2*G*s on the *G* Meter. Use the Flight Path Marker in the HUD to get to 60 degrees. To get a better reference for 60 degrees, you can press SHIFT-F2 and take a look at your bank angle from the Chase Plane View.

During this turn, drag the Flight Path Marker straight across the horizon so you will maintain level flight. Keep 2*G*s on the jet using back stick pressure and use bank angle to control the Flight Path Marker.

If you are using a keyboard to fly the jet, you'll need to move your fingers rapidly to execute this turn. When flying the F-19 with the keyboard, it helps to be a piccolo player. If you're not a piccolo player, just keep practicing until you can move your fingers like one.

As you make this turn, notice the Heading Scale at the top of the HUD move. Try to roll out on a heading of south (180 degrees). To do this you will have to start your roll out between 3 and 5 degrees prior to reaching the desired heading.

You will notice when executing this turn that you did not need to input very much, if any, back stick pressure (using the ↓ key). That's because back stick pressure is automatically applied by the F-19 flight controls when you roll into a bank. The amount of back stick pressure or *pitch* commanded is directly related to your bank angle. This pitch input based on bank angle makes flying the jet around the sky easier but presents some real challenges in air-to-air combat when you get into a nose pointing contest. Since nose pointing with jets is one of my favorite subjects, we will thoroughly discuss F-19 techniques for doing it in Chapter 5.

For now just keep practicing low *G* turns until you get a feel for how much back stick pressure is required for level turns. Once you've got it down, start trying climbing and descending turns. To execute these, use the stick or ↓/↑ to place the Flight Path Marker above and below the horizon (for climbing and diving, respectively). By practicing these types of turns you will get a "feel" for the jet.

When you have had enough practice move on to high G turns.

High G Turns

All high G turns in the F-19 have one thing in common: they are very short in duration. The F-19 is a real pig under high G and sheds airspeed very quickly. As the airspeed bleeds off, the G available goes down and you will eventually stall the aircraft. For this reason, don't expect to stay in a high G turn in the F-19 for very long.

To perform a high G turn, first go to full power by hitting the = key. Roll the aircraft into a 75-85 degree bank with the joystick or the ← or → key, and start applying G with the joystick or ↓ key. Keep pulling Gs until the G Meter gets to 8Gs. When the airspeed bleeds off to 350 knots roll out

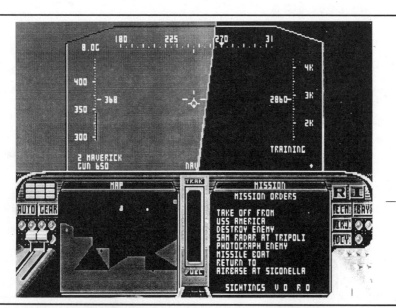

Figure 3-19. High G turn

of the turn. You can see how fast this jet slows down. High *G* turns are important in the F-19 but you have to carefully monitor your knots. Figure 3-19 shows the F-19 in a high *G* turn.

I'm sure you noticed that you needed very little back stick pressure to pull 8*G*s at 75 to 85 degrees. Again, the aircraft automatically pulls into the turn as you roll. To see how many *G*s are commanded at various bank angles, set the Flight Path Marker on the horizon and change bank angle without adding any back stick pressure. Notice the *G* Meter in HUD change in response to new bank angles.

Stalls

We discussed earlier in the chapter why an aircraft stalls. It is now time to practice stall recoveries. In order to do this we first have to get into a stall. To set up for the stall, climb the jet up to 3,000 feet and turn toward the north.

Low-Speed Stalls

Pull the power back to 33 percent of maximum (one-third of the way back). The airspeed will rapidly bleed off. Keep pulling back on the stick to keep the aircraft in level flight (the Flight Path Marker should be on the horizon). By watching the difference between the Gun Cross and the Flight Path Marker, you will notice that the aircraft AOA keeps increasing. At about 130 knots, the Stall Indicator line reaches the Airspeed Marker and a stall warning message appears in the HUD. Keep holding back stick pressure and notice that even with full aft stick commanded you cannot hold level flight. The airspeed will stabilize at about 65 knots and the Flight Path Marker will be below the horizon. In this condition you have passed the jet's maximum AOA and are losing lift. Figure 3-20 shows the F-19 in a low-speed stall.

When you descend between 2,000 and 2,500 feet, recover from the stall by going full power, *rolling wings level,* and centering the stick. When you reach 200 knots start a slow pull out. F-19 pilots that have flown light aircraft know that a stall causes the nose in those types of aircraft to abruptly fall off like a light aircraft. Aircraft with swept wings (such as the

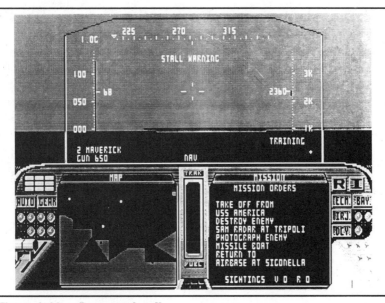

Figure 3-20.   Low-speed stall

Stealth Fighter) stall with their nose in a more upright position. If you center the stick at any time during the stall in the F-19, it will self recover eventually. A pilot can recover from a stall much faster than the auto recovery logic so don't bet your rear end on the little white mice in the flight control system. Recover the jet yourself.

High-Speed Stalls

A high-speed stall is completely different from a low-speed stall. In a high-speed stall, the aircraft is under G; to break the stall all you have to do is relax the G and accelerate. Climb back up to 3,000 feet to set up for a high-speed stall.

   To enter the stall, go to maximum power, accelerate to 450 knots, and roll the jet into 75 to 85 degrees of bank. Next pull back on the stick to start a 6 to 8 G turn. Keep pulling until the Stall Indicator rises up to the airspeed marker. When you get a stall warning in the HUD, center the stick to release the G.

Remember from our low *G* training that you must roll the wings level in the F-19 to release all of the back stick pressure. Thus, there is a two-step procedure in the F-19 to recover from a high-speed stall. First, center the stick, and second, roll the wings level. After you gain at least 50 knots of airspeed, roll the wings back into a more gentle bank angle and reapply the *G* smoothly but do not let the Stall Indicator reach the airspeed mark. If it starts to approach the mark, ease off the *G* by reducing your bank and back stick pressure.

You are probably wondering why we are not accelerating to our original airspeed before we reapply the *G*. In a combat situation you are doing a high *G* turn for a purpose. Your life may depend on you staying in the turn, so if you find yourself in a stall you may not have the luxury of gaining back all of your original knots. This recovery procedure will keep you in the turn and, as much as possible, in the fight.

LANDING THE F-19

Recently I was leading a two-ship flight of A-7s back to the field to land. My wingman had lost his radio so he needed to land on my wing. We configured normally (with gear and flaps down), set up on the ILS, and at the five-mile point we started down the glide path. When we reached 300 feet I still couldn't see the runway so I was starting to think about going around when suddenly the runway took shape off in the mist. I lined up quickly on what I could see of the runway and kept coming down. As I got closer I noticed that something was not right. Just then my wingman said, "hey lead, are we really going to land on the taxiway?" As he was talking, I realized that we were lined up on the parallel taxiway and not the runway. I quickly steered the formation over to the "real runway" and executed a decent lead formation landing—decent considering I was somewhat flustered and embarrassed by my gross buffoonery.

Every year, experienced pilots mess up a simple landing pattern by doing something stupid (like landing on a taxiway). Landing the jet is easy once you get in the groove but you must stay alert and not get complacent. Murphy and his irrefutable Law are lurking around the field for any pilot who has incorrectly assumed that the mission was over after leaving the target area.

Landing the jet safely is one of the most satisfying accomplishments in the F-19 simulation. There are plenty of successful ways to get the jet on the ground or on the deck of the ship. I will give you my technique, which is very straightforward and easy to do.

To get set up for the landing we first have to steer for the airstrip at Sigonella. To do this, press F7 to call up the Waypoint screen on the right MFD. Next, hold down the SHIFT key and press PGDN until the last waypoint on the list is highlighted.

Since we are not going into the target area, we will step past the other waypoints on the list and select waypoint 4, the airfield at Sigonella. The waypoint steering mark on the Heading Scale in the HUD will now guide us to the airfield. We can turn the jet to line up on this heading, or we can select the autopilot by hitting the **7** key. With the autopilot engaged, the jet automatically steers toward the selected waypoint. We are now heading for the field and ready to enter the landing pattern. The following steps will take you through the landing procedure:

1. Drive straight for the field until you reach 50 kilometers.

2. At 50 kilometers, reduce the power to 50 percent and climb or descend to 2,000 feet.

3. The airfield is now on your nose, so go into the NAV mode in the HUD by hitting F2 until "NAV" appears in the bottom of the HUD. Next, press F9 to call up the ILS. With the ILS called up you will get a horizontal and vertical bar in the HUD that will provide you with azimuth (left/right lineup) and glide slope (up/down lineup) information for landing.

4. All runways in the F-19 simulation are oriented 00/180 or north/south. You can land going either direction on a runway but can only land to the south on an aircraft carrier. To help orient yourself to the runway, press F3 to call up an overhead tactical display on the left MFD. As a further aid, call up the F-19 forward-looking optical sensor by pressing the / key. The sensor will lock-on to the runway at Sigonella and provide you with a magnfied view of the field in the right MFD.

5. Using the tactical display on the left MFD, project a point on the map at least on grid square straight south of the runway, and steer for this point.

6. At 20 kilometers bring the power back to 33 percent and drop the gear (with the **6** key) and the flaps (with the **9** key), and set the power at 33 to 50 percent to hold 150-200 knots.

7. When you reach the point that you have projected south of the runway, or you see from your optical display in the right MFD that you are lined up for landing, start following the ILS steering bars. *Do not follow the ILS steering bars until you are within 10 degrees of the runway heading.* If you do, the ILS will command you to turn toward the runway and will bring you in on an angling final. Always project the runway center line out to about 15 kilometers, and then drive to this point until the HUD Steering Cue is within 10 degrees of runway heading. When this occurs, follow the ILS steering bars. The jet should be at 150-200 knots.

   To follow the ILS, turn the jet with shallow bank angles to line up the Vertical ILS Steering Line with the vertical lines of the Gun Cross. The Horizontal ILS Steering Line gives you the glide path, and once you are inside 10 kilometers it should start to descend through the Gun Cross to indicate that you are on the glide path. Reduce power by pressing the – key once, and start a gradual descent to follow the ILS Glide Path Indicator. To start your descent, place the Flight Path Marker slightly below the horizon and adjust the position of the horizontal ILS Pitch Bar to keep it centered on the horizontal Gun Cross lines. Figure 3-21 shows this position on the glide path.

8. You should now see the runway clearly. Once you do, you can line up and make final azimuth corrections. *Keep flying the ILS glide path until you can see the runway well enough to place your Flight Path Marker on it.* Figure 3-22 shows the jet's position 4 kilometers out with the Flight Path Marker on the runway. Don't let the Flight Path Marker drift off the runway once you get in close.

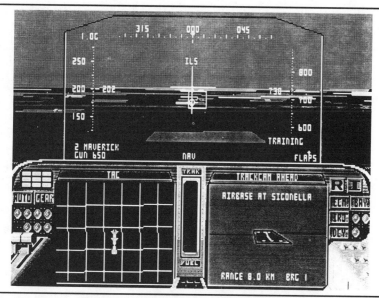

Figure 3-21.   HUD view of landing from 8 kilometers

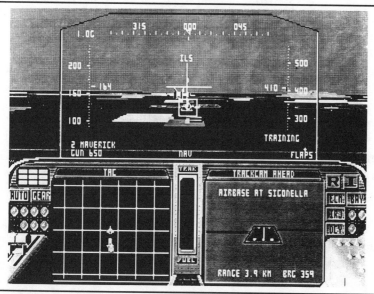

Figure 3-22.   HUD view of landing from 3.9 kilometers

9. As you approach the runway threshold, press the **9** key to extend the speedbrakes and slow down to 140-150 knots. As the altitude in the HUD approaches 0, pull back gently on the stick to slow your descent (VVI). The VVI Indicator is very difficult to use when you're in the flare; if you are going to check your rate of descent do it prior to 4 kilometers on final. The only thing you need to cross-check inside of 4 kilometers is runway and airspeed—runway for line up and airspeed for stall. Don't bother looking at the stall indicator—just check that you stay above 130 knots. Remember, inside 4 kilometers it's "runway/airspeed, runway/airspeed," all the way down.

10. When you touch down, be sure the brakes are still on, pull the power to idle, and steer toward the center of the runway with the joystick or the ← or → keys.

Carrier Landings

You can use this same procedure for landing on a carrier with a few exceptions. The first is you must land on a carrier to the south. There are no arresting wires on the other end of the boat and you will also interfere with the launch cycle. Another difference is you do not flare the aircraft. You drive the F-19 straight down to touch down with the power set. You must touch down prior to one of the three arresting wires or you will *bolter* (miss the wires). When this happens you must go full power up, and go around and try again. When you get close to the deck while doing a carrier landing, make sure that the Flight Path Marker is positioned near the middle of the three wires. When you touch down, go full power until you are sure that you have taken a wire.

To practice carrier landings, exit the simulation by holding down ALT and pressing **Q**. Reenter the simulation and set the same mission variable. This time after takeoff, however, turn north, and set up for a practice landing on the carrier. Use the same ranges and techniques for line-up that you did for a runway landing.

MISSION DEBRIEFING

You will never reach your full potential as an F-19 fighter pilot until you master the basics. The F-19 is an easy aircraft to fly but a tough jet to master in air combat. Stalls and landings must be second nature to you in order to be able to go on to the more complex task of destroying the enemy.

4

F-19 Weapons

"No weapon is too short for a brave man"
Ancient proverb used to describe the A-7 fighter

It turned out to be the kind of day that dreams are made of—nightmares, to be more specific. Of course when I arrived at the squadron for my flight briefing, I had no idea that this flight would make me famous. Unfortunately it was the kind of fame that we all strive to avoid.

It was a typical Las Vegas spring day, and the sky was clear and bright. I was attending the F-16 Weapons School, and today's mission was a two-ship sortie up to the bombing range north of Nellis Air Force Base for a live CBU drop. Before we get any further into the gory details, I'd better describe the U.S. Air Force Fighter Weapons School to put this whole story in perspective.

The Weapons School is a four-month test of manhood, held at Nellis Air Force Base three times a year. The Weapons School is the center of learning for all advanced fighter weapons and tactics. It does not teach absolute truths about fighter tactics (since none exist). Rather it teaches fighter fundamentals and tested methods for approaching tactical problems (not the specific solutions to these problems).

Fighter pilots are selected from around the world to attend the school, and upon graduation they return to their squadrons to bring back the word from the mountain. Instead of stone tablets, the Fighter Weapons Officer returns with a *tactical perspective*—a fundamental knowledge of his own aircraft, the enemy threat, and how to approach destroying one with the other.

This course is a deadly serious business, and no prisoners are taken. To combat this four-month onslaught, a fighter pilot needs to be armed with a thick skin and a short memory. This intense program is a challenge to even the best fighter pilots. You will be knocked down in this program. The trick is to get up, shake it off, and get back in the fight. Like most other pursuits in life, at the Weapons School you must learn from your mistakes without being paralyzed by them.

Anyway, back to the story. The scenario for the mission was straightforward. A convoy of enemy trucks was stuck along a north/south road 10 miles behind the Forward Edge of the Battle Area (FEBA). Our job was to attack and destroy this convoy with CBU bombs. CBUs are a canistered munition. Several hundred softball-sized bomblets are packed in a canister that looks like a bomb. When this bomb is dropped, it falls until the fuze functions. When the fuze functions, the bomb casing opens like a clam shell and the bomblets are released to rain down on the target. Some of the bomblets (also called *submunitions*) detonate on contact while others lie on the ground and go off at random intervals. This weapon was introduced in the Vietnam War, and the North Vietnamese soon learned to stay clear of the curious little balls that were left behind after a CBU attack. An F-16 normally carries four of these bombs, and with a single attack can make life very unpleasant over a 200-600 square-foot area. The actual target for our attack on this day was a column of old trucks on the bombing range. This target array was specially built for live CBU drops.

The primary enemy threat on this mission was two Navy A-4 Aggressor aircraft that were protecting the target. I was flying this mission with an instructor named Skip. He was a great all- around jet driver and a good instructor except for one particular problem. Just about every time I flew with this guy on an air-to-ground ride I messed something up. This day was no exception.

Takeoff and ingress into the target area were smooth and uneventful. Approaching the target area, however, things changed: I picked up a single bandit on my radar, low and coming at our flight at high speed. After calling out the target I went outside the cockpit to check Skip's six o'clock. As I came back inside to check the target on the radar, Skip picked up an A-4 visually at my seven o'clock. He called for me to break left, and I quickly pulled the jet around in an 8G turn to meet the attacker. I passed the A-4 canopy to canopy at high aspect and continued the turn to keep him in sight. Skip turned hard also to get his nose on the bandit, and fired a Sidewinder (simulated, of course). He kept turning on the bandit and called "engaged offensive" while I rolled out of my turn and started searching visually for the other bandit that I knew was closing on the fight. Skip quickly got behind the A-4 and "fired" another Sidewinder, ending the fight. On this sortie we had briefed a two-shot kill rule, which meant that when you were hit twice you had to leave the fight for 30 seconds. After 30 seconds you could regenerate and return to the fight.

With this bandit dead and out of the fight, we quickly got back into one-mile, line abreast formation and headed for the target. We still had not found the other bandit but knew he had probably found us and was waiting for the right moment to attack. We arrived at the Initial Point (IP) for our CBU attack and armed up the bombs. At four miles from the target we checked 30 degrees right for offset from the target and started our element pop-up attack. Just as I started to pull up, I sighted the other A-4 at Skip's six o'clock, closing. I called for Skip to break, and started a high G turn to get my nose on the bandit. Skip turned tight and avoided being hosed by the A-4, and I quickly got off a high-aspect Sidewinder shot on the bandit. I passed the A-4 close aboard, left to left, and check-turned to keep a tally. He didn't set his wings for a turn and blew straight through the fight. I called for Skip to join back up in formation for the planned CBU attack. I knew the other A-4 (that we'd already killed) would be closing in on the fight. I wanted to execute the CBU attack before he showed up. Also the A-4 we had just shot was not dead (since we only got off one shot on him) and could turn back into us at any time. I switched my weapon system back to air-to-ground and started to pop. As I climbed above 4,000 feet I spotted the truck convoy and rolled in for the attack.

Skip had been sucked into a trail position by all of this maneuvering and was gamely trying to catch up and execute the attack. As I dove down on the target, I noticed that my Target Locator Line was showing the target about 2 miles to the south of where I was attacking. It is not unusual for this to happen since I had not had time to update my weapon system before the attack; this could be just a normal drift error. When the pipper got to the target I hit the pickle button. At the same second that I released the bombs Skip came on the radio and yelled, "DON'T DROP!"

Later when I recalled this moment, a line from an old song came to mind. In the song a man takes his wife to various places, and everywhere he goes a male "streaker" appears. In this part of the song he is at a basketball game and it happens again. He shouts, "Don't look Ethel." Then he forlornly states, "But it was too late. She already got a free shot."

Well, unless God quickly repealed the Law of Gravity it was also "too late" to stop these bombs. Since there was no supernatural intervention, down they fell, right toward the target. At fuze function altitude my concern multiplied as the bomb clam shells opened, releasing hundreds of submunitions. When they reached the earth, the ground erupted in bright sparkles as the bomblets detonated. Up to this point I knew that something bad was going to happen because of Skip's desperate radio call, but all I could do was watch and worry because I still didn't know why he had made the call.

As the explosions pattern started to move north, the problem became crystal clear. I had attacked the northernmost section of the target array instead of the center. By doing this, the top part of the submunition pattern had covered an east/west road that ran near the northernmost part of the target column. This road was used by military vehicles that worked on the range, and although they didn't travel on it when aircraft were bombing, it was used frequently at other times. I knew that it would take a very long time to find, sweep, and disarm the submunitions that hit the road. I also knew that I was in big trouble. Skip and I terminated the mission and circled the area to join up and return to the base.

After landing I was immediately summoned to the squadron commander's office where I was given the opportunity to describe the mission. The squadron commander listened silently without interrupting until I had finished. He then said, "I'm sure you know that you are going to repeat this ride." I answered, "Yes sir," I did. He added a few more choice words, that I'll leave out for the sake of decency, and told me to get out of his office. As I got to the door he said, "Don't expect to drop any more CBUs in my squadron. You'll have to fly this ride again with practice bombs. Consider yourself lucky I'm even giving you those." I left the squadron commander's office surprised and relieved that I didn't wash out of the program.

This mission taught me two important lessons. The first one is that you must study the target area in detail. The CBU targets for this mission were very easy to see so I didn't bother to commit the target area to memory. If I had, I would have realized during the attack that I was bombing the northern part of the convoy.

The second lesson learned is to know the weapons that you are using. I was so accustomed to dropping single 25lb practice bombs that I didn't realize just how big a CBU pattern can be and the danger of not being precise. I will remember the sight of those bombs drifting toward the ground and my feeling of helplessness for a long time. Once you hit the pickle button and let those babies go, there is no way to hit the rewind switch and recall them. You have to do it right the first time.

As a seasoned F-19 pilot, I know you have experienced missions that were very similar to the one just described. Air combat presents the fighter pilot with a dazzling series of rapid-fire choices, and the F-19 simulation captures and recreates this environment. Not knowing my weapons played at least a part in the problems I encountered during my CBU mission. This chapter will teach you what you need to know about your weapons so you can avoid weapons-related mistakes in the F-19 air war. In this chapter, we will discuss how weapons work, which targets they are effective against, and what type of HUD symbology is associated with each weapon. In a later chapter, once you have the basics down, we will discuss techniques for air-to-air and air-to-ground weapons employment.

WHITE SMOCKS AND WINDOWLESS BUILDINGS

The F-19 enters the air combat arena with a single purpose: Execute the mission and survive. To execute the mission the pilot has a wide range of weapons choices. In order to make these choices, the F-19 pilot must understand how each weapon works and what target it is designed to kill.

In F-19 there is a very long list of what I call "designer weapons"—weapons that are customized for specific targets. Examples of these are the Penguin missile for ships and the Durandal bomb for runways. Out in the real-world where the rubber meets the road there are very few of these exotic weapons. Most of the weapons in the bomb dumps around the world are plain vanilla, general-purpose bombs. These bombs have not changed very much since Billy Mitchell sank the *Ostfriesland*. What has changed is the accuracy with which a modern fighter can deliver them.

A general-purpose bomb is good for almost any target if you can hit it. Since the weapon is going to blow up and cannot be reused, the more expensive and exotic you make a weapon, the less of them you are going to have in the fight. By contrast a dumb bomb is cheap, and if dropped by a smart airplane (one with advanced sensors and computers), it is also accurate.

Designer weapons are still very important to the fighter pilot even though they are usually in short supply. The F-19 gives the pilot a chance to employ these weapons in simulated combat and by so doing gain an insight into modern weaponry. These weapons are designed in labs that are hidden away in nondescript, windowless buildings around the country. You can sometimes spot the guys that work in these labs. They normally have their front shirt pocket full of pens and pencils, a calculator clipped to their belt, and a general disheveled appearance. These are the guys that dream up stuff like CBUs and HARM missiles, and I say "God bless them." When it's your own rear end on the line, you need the best technology possible to do the mission (even though you may not want the guys who develop this technology to date your sister).

AIR-TO-GROUND WEAPONS

There are two general categories of weapons. Weapons that are precision guided by their own onboard avionics (smart weapons) and weapons that the aircraft must aim (dumb weapons). Smart weapons may be powered, as in the case of missiles, or may be unpowered, such as laser-guided bombs. All dumb weapons in the F-19 are free-fall bombs (with the exception of the 20-mm gun). Dumb bombs can be further divided into high-drag and low-drag types. Normally the high-drag designator does not apply to cluster type munitions, but for the purpose of our discussion we will lump these types of weapons in with the true high-drag general-purpose bombs. The reason for this is that in the F-19, canistered weapons and finned, high-drag weapons have roughly the same ballistics and aiming cues. In this chapter we will discuss air-to-ground weapons and avionics first, since in the F-19 simulation they are more complex and numerous.

Air-to-Ground Sensors

Before we start our discussion of air-to-ground weapons, we will first discuss F-19 sensors and displays. The most important of these is the Forward Looking Infrared/Optics (FLIR/Optics) sensor. This sensor is also called a tracking camera. You activate this sensor by hitting the / key. After you press this key the sensor searches directly in front of the aircraft and locks on to the first target that it finds.

The type of target that the sensor searches for and locks on to is controlled by which HUD mode the you select. You change the HUD modes by pressing the F2 key. To place the HUD in the air-to-air mode, press the F2 key until the words "AIR-AIR" appear in the bottom of the HUD.

In the air-to-air HUD mode the FLIR/Optics sensor will only lock-on to aircraft targets. With the HUD in the air-to-ground mode, the FLIR/Optics sensor locks on to ground targets, and with the HUD in the "Nav" mode it only locks on to runways.

After lock-on to a target, a magnified target image is displayed on the right Multifunctional Display (MFD) in the cockpit along with a print of the bearing and range to the target. Figure 4-1 shows a cockpit view of the right MFD with the FLIR/Optics sensor locked on to a missile boat. If you call up the Tactical (Tac) Display on the left MFD by pressing the F3 key, you will see a grid-lined overhead view of the battle. In the center of the display, a small F-19 icon will appear along with icons representing all other relevant battlefield entities that are around the aircraft. After the FLIR/Optics sensor locks on to a target, a box will appear around the target icon on the Tac Display corresponding to the target that is locked on and displayed on the right MFD. Figure 4-2 shows the left MFD Tac Display with a Target Designator (TD) box around the same ship that is being displayed on the right MFD.

Along with the target picture on the right MFD, the pilot also gets a brief target description (such as bridge, barracks, missile boat, and so on). If the target is the primary or secondary target for the mission, the MFD

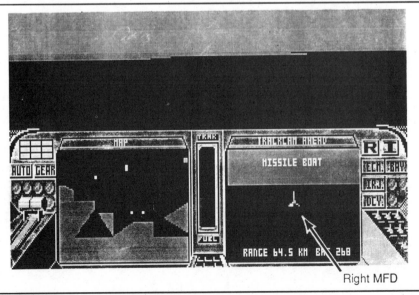

Right MFD

Figure 4-1.   FLIR/Optics Sensor Display in right MFD

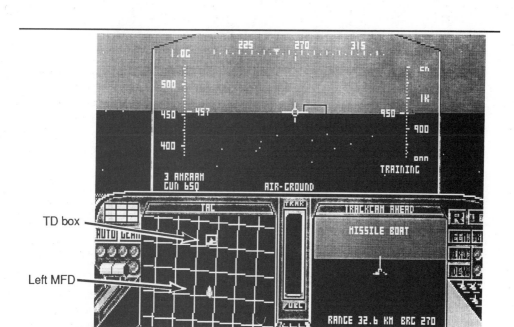

Figure 4-2. Tac Display on the left MFD with TD box on the missile boat

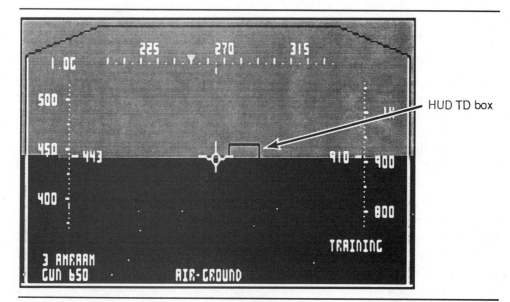

Figure 4-3. TD box display in the HUD

will print out "primary/secondary target" directly under the target description. Along with these target displays on the right and left MFD, a TD box will appear in the HUD around the locked on target. Figure 4-3 shows the HUD Target Designator box around this same missile boat target.

In addition to searching directly in front of the jet, this sensor can be commanded to search to the left, right, or rear of the aircraft. The following keys are used to execute each of these commands:

Search left	**M** key
Search right	**,** key
Search rear	**.** key

In addition, these same keys can be used by the pilot to get an out-the-cockpit view. This is accomplished by pressing the SHIFT key along with the key corresponding to the direction out of the cockpit that the pilot wishes to look. SHIFT-M will give the pilot a view to the left, SHIFT-, will give the pilot a view out of the cockpit to the right, and SHIFT-. will let the pilot view directly behind the jet.

Avoiding Finger Flail

There are two more important FLIR/Optics controls. These are the **B** and **N** keys. The **B** key returns the sensor to the search mode in the previously designated search area (ahead of the jet, to the right, and so on). It can then lock-on to a new target in this area. If there is not another target in this area then the sensor will re-lock the same target. Pressing any of the previously listed controls will cause the sensor to lock-on to only the targets that are stored in the F-19 weapons computer memory. These are the important military targets in the area for that mission.

If you wish to search for other targets that are not in the computer's memory, press the **N** key. The FLIR/Optics sensor will now search for these other targets, lock-on to them, and then store them in the computer's memory. *You must be very careful with this key.* The computer only has limited memory. If you have previously hit the **B** key on an important target and then hit the **N** key to search for new targets, the new target may replace the important target in the computer's memory. You may get into a real finger flail on the keyboard trying to get your FLIR/Optics sensor locked on to the desired target. To avoid this, don't use the **N** key until you have at least accomplished your primary mission (unless you are very sure of what you are doing).

The "Shoot Stupid" Cue

One of the most important functions of the FLIR/Optics sensor is to provide the pilot with an indication that a selected air-to-air or air-to-ground missile is locked on to the target. When the selected weapon is locked on to the target, a flashing "Missile Lock" indication is flashed across the screen, and a cross appears over the target in the right MFD. Figure 4-4 shows this Missile Lock Display. In the HUD, around the designated target, the TD box changes to an oval shape when the weapon locks on to the target. This indication is depicted in Figure 4-5.

    All these indicators can be used to cue the pilot that the weapon is locked on and in range. Instead of a flashing "Missile Lock" message,

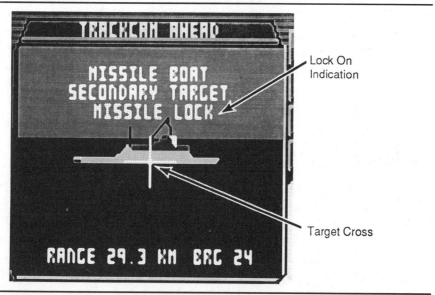

Figure 4-4. Missile Lock Display in the right MFD

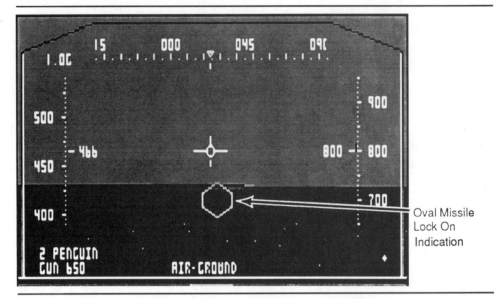

Figure 4-5. Oval Missile Lock-On Indication in the HUD

replace the words "Missile Lock" in your mind with the words "shoot stupid." This is the *maximum* range that you can launch the weapon at the target but it is not necessarily the *optimum* range to release the weapon. All fighters have maximum range "shoot stupid" cues and the F-19 is no exception. It is up to the fighter pilot, however, to know his weapon—when to shoot is based on more than just a maximum range "shoot stupid" indication.

Air-to-Ground Missiles

The air-to-ground missiles used in the F-19 simulation are the Penguin, Harpoon, Maverick, and HARM. These missiles are all *launch and leave*. Simply stated this means that once the missile is fired toward the target with a lock-on, it no longer requires guidance assistance from the launching aircraft. This gives the fighter freedom to maneuver after firing the missile. Figure 4-6 shows all four of these missiles.

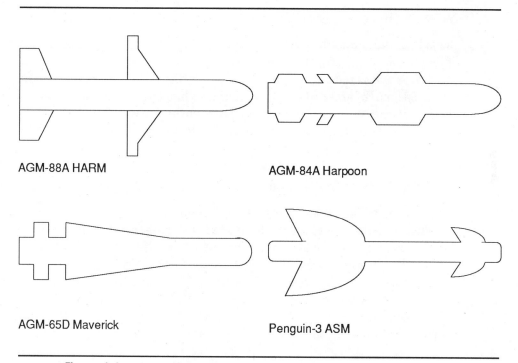

AGM-88A HARM

AGM-84A Harpoon

AGM-65D Maverick

Penguin-3 ASM

Figure 4-6. Air-to-Ground Missiles

Penguin-3 ASM Missile

The Penguin is an anti-ship missile that was designed for use in the narrow fjords of Norway. This environment is characterized by narrow bodies of water shielded by steep cliffs. This type of environment makes radar-guided anti-ship missiles useless because of the severe radar clutter problems caused by the mountains that bound the fjords. The Norwegians overcame this problem by making the Penguin Infrared (IR) guided. The missile can also be used in the open ocean; its small size and great accuracy make it an excellent weapon. In the F-19 simulation it is used exclusively to attack ships but it is slightly less effective than the Harpoon. Maximum range is 32 kilometers.

AGM-84 Harpoon Missile

This U.S.-built anti-ship missile was one of the first missiles designed for this role, and it is still the best missile in the world against ships in the open ocean. It is radar-guided and extremely difficult to jam or decoy. The missile is much larger than a Penguin but it has much better range and a bigger warhead. It is the most effective anti-ship weapon in the F-19 simulation, with a maximum range of 60 kilometers.

AGM-65D Maverick Missile

The "D" model Maverick is a tank-killing missile that can also be used effectively against most vertically developed targets that emit heat. These targets can be identified by their *heat signature* (the areas and intensity of heat the target emits that are specific to the target). *Vertical development* simply means it sticks up above the ground. The real missile is worthless against bridges and oil storage tanks because they are not hot targets and the missile has an Imaging Infrared (IIR) guidance system. In the F-19 simulation, however, the missile is the most flexible air-to-ground weapon you can carry. It is good against almost all targets in the F-19 simulation including bridges, and has a 32 kilometer range. It is not an effective weapon, however, against submarine pens or other below-ground targets. In a real single-seat fighter this weapon is a real handful to employ effectively because there is no auto-lock feature on the missile. The pilot must find the target and manually slew the seeker head of the Maverick over to the target and lock-on. In the F-19 all of this is done automatically, making the Maverick a very easy-to-use weapon.

AGM-88A HARM

The High-speed Anti-Radiation Missile is one of the finest weapons in our inventory. This missile homes in on enemy radars and overcomes most of the significant limitations of its predecessor, the AGM-45 Shrike. The HARM is very fast (Mach2+) and can remember the position of an enemy radar even after it shuts down. In the F-19 simulation it can be used against both ground-based and ship-born radars and is a very powerful weapon.

The maximum range of the missile is 20 kilometers in this simulation, which is not realistic. The real HARM is a more potent weapon.

Air-to-Ground Missile (AGM) Symbology

All of these missiles are fired using the same cockpit weapons symbology. You enter the air-to-ground HUD mode by pressing the F2 key until the words "AIR-GROUND" appear at the bottom of the HUD. You then hit the SPACEBAR to cycle through all the weapons that are loaded in the bomb bays. As you press the SPACEBAR, the weapon names at the bottom-right corner of the HUD will change along with the weapon's HUD aiming symbology.

For the weapons we have discussed, you first lock-on the FLIR/Optics sensor, which gives you a TD box in the HUD over the selected target. Figure 4-7 shows this basic AGM symbology. When you get within maximum missile range, this box changes to an oval.

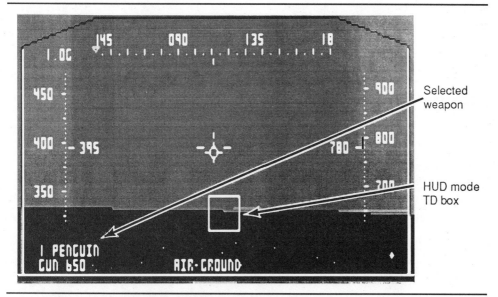

Figure 4-7.   Pre-Lock-On HUD Missile Symbology

Laser-Guided Bombs

Laser-guided bombs are smart, precision-guided weapons. These bombs have a laser guidance kit fitted to the front part of the bomb that picks up reflected laser energy that is being shined on the target by either the attacking aircraft or another aircraft in the flight. When the bomb "sees" the laser, it guides to the target by way of small fins located on a guidance kit in the front of the bomb. These weapons are not powered and the aircraft releasing them must get close in order for the bomb to reach the target. In the F-19 simulation there are three laser-guided weapons: the GBU-12 Paveway, the CBU-72 FAE, and the Mk-20 Rockeye II. Only the GBU-12 is a real-world laser-guided weapon. Figure 4-8 shows all three of these F-19 laser-guided bombs.

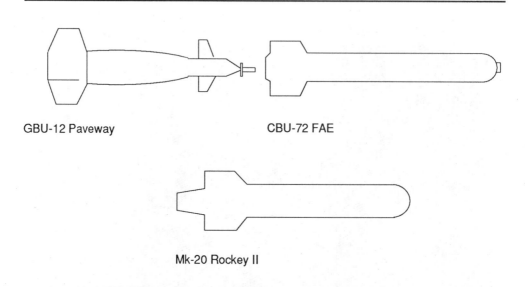

GBU-12 Paveway   CBU-72 FAE

Mk-20 Rockey II

Figure 4-8.   Laser-guided bombs

GBU-12 Paveway

The GBU-12 Paveway is an Mk-82 500lb general-purpose bomb fitted with a laser guidance kit in the nose. The 2000lb version of this bomb was used by the F-111s in the attack against Libya. In order for the bomb to guide, a Pave Tack laser designator pod tracks the target to provide reflected energy for the bomb to home-in on. The GBU-12 Paveway is a good weapon for almost all targets. It is very effective against bridges and bunkers where precision is mandatory. In the F-19 simulation it is effective against virtually the same targets that it is used for in the real world. All above-ground structures are vulnerable to this bomb. In the simulation the bomb has 2 kilometers of range for every 1,000 feet of F-19 altitude.

CBU-72 FAE

This weapon is unique to the F-19 simulation. Fuel Air Explosive bombs were used in Vietnam but have since gone out of the inventory. With an FAE bomb, heavy explosive gases are released when the bomb hits the ground. These gases settle down into open bunkers or other exposed structures. The gas is then ignited, creating a destructive overpressure. In the simulation this weapon is used to destroy submarine pens and buildings. It has the same range limits as the GBU-12 Paveway.

Mk-20 Rockeye II

Rockeye is a real canistered weapon that drops dart-like submunitions designed to attack armored vehicles (described shortly). Rockeye II is not a real-world laser-guided weapon, but in the F-19 simulation it can be used to kill all above-ground targets except bridges.

Laser-Guided Bomb Symbology

In the F-19, Laser-Guided Bomb Symbology is the same as the AGM symbology. Figure 4-9 shows the HUD and right MFD FLIR/Optics picture

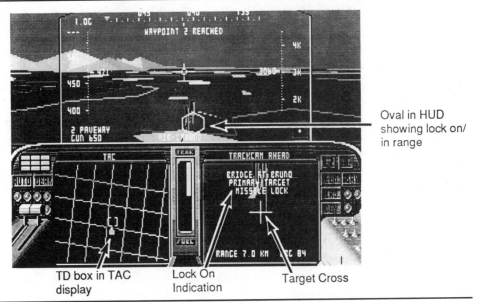

Figure 4-9.   Laser-Guided Bomb Symbology at lock-on

for an in-range release of a GBU-12 Paveway. You will notice that the symbology is the same as the AGM cues.

High-Drag Bombs

High-drag bombs have either fins, air bags, or parachutes to slow them down. These devices are added to the bomb in most cases to allow the release aircraft to escape the *frag* or fragmentation from the bomb explosion. The Durandal runway cratering bomb is the exception to this rule and has a parachute to stabilize the bomb in a vertical position in order to get the maximum runway penetration. For the purpose of our discussion we are also calling the canistered munitions high-drag bombs. This is not really true since these weapons are not retarded in any way. They do, however, have a short bomb range similar to the retarded weapons, and in the F-19 simulation they use the same HUD release symbology. The reason they have such a short bomb range is that they only fall like a bomb for a

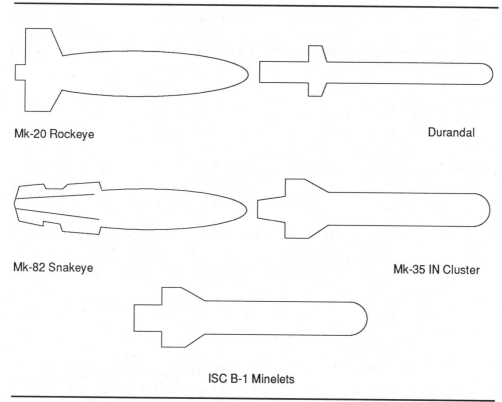

Figure 4-10.   High-drag bombs

short distance before opening and releasing their submunitions. As soon as these bombs open up they lose a lot of forward speed and have a corresponding shorter bomb range. All real-world high-drag bombs are just as accurate as low-drag bombs. These bombs are shown in Figure 4-10.

Mk-20 Rockeye

The Rockeye is a canistered munition that was originally designed to kill armored vehicles. It works precisely like the CBU bomb I described in the story at the beginning of this chapter. Instead of softball-sized bomblets, however, the Rockeye submunitions look like large darts. These submunitions have fins, a long nose, and possess an armor-piercing warhead. This weapon is good against vehicles, radars, and other light structures in both real-world battles and the simulation.

Durandal

This weapon is used to crater runways. After release from the aircraft, a parachute deploys, stabilizing the weapon in a vertical position. A radar sensor in the nose of the bomb detects function height, and at this point a rocket motor fires to propel the warhead deep within the runway. The fuze functions at this time, detonating the bomb and causing a big hole. Destroying runways is really just destroying concrete. This is a very tough task. In addition, fixing a runway is not particularly time-consuming or difficult, making attacking runways an even more frustrating endeavor. Both in the real-world and in the simulation, the Durandal is the only weapon for the job.

Mk-82 Snakeye

The Mk-82 Snakeye is a 500lb general-purpose bomb with a high- drag air bag attached to the rear of the bomb. This bomb is currently, and therefore more correctly, called Mk-82 AIR. After release from the aircraft, the air bag deploys, slowing the bomb and allowing the attacker to escape the frag pattern. The Snake is a very flexible weapon and is effective for all above-ground targets. In the F-19 simulation the bomb is good against these same targets. There are two reasons why I like the Mk-82 AIR: you can drop it at very low altitudes, and it is effective against virtually any target on the battlefield.

Mk-35 IN Cluster

This bomb is a notional F-19 canistered weapon that is patterned after the CBU bomb described at the beginning of the chapter. This weapon has incendiary submunitions that cause fires, and is effective against all above-ground targets except bridges.

ISC B-1 Minelets

This is another notional F-19 canistered weapon that has submunitions almost identical to the real-world CBU bomb. In the F-19 simulation this weapon is good against runways. It does not destroy them—it just halts flight operations until they are cleared. It is also a good weapon against light structures such as radars and buildings.

High-Drag Bomb Symbology

With all of the high-drag bombs described, the attacking aircraft must overfly the target. There are only two aiming cues required for these bombs, and they are both in the HUD. The first of these is an aiming diamond that provides the pilot azimuth steering. The next indicator is a ranging bar that starts to shrink as the pilot gets closer to the target. Both of these cues are depicted in Figure 4-11.

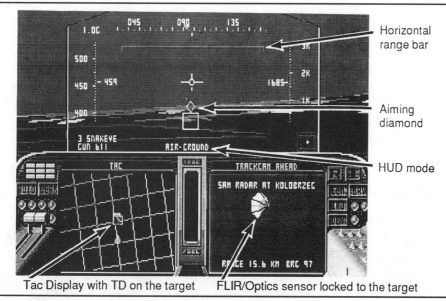

Figure 4-11.   High-Drag Bomb Symbology

Low-Drag Bombs

I saved the easiest air-to-ground weapon until last. The low-drag bomb is just a bomb. You fly over the target and drop it—no parachutes pop out, no fins or canisters pop open, and no magic eyes search for the target. The bomb just falls to the ground and goes boom. This is a pure and simple dumb bomb. The two types of low-drag bombs that are used by the F-19 are the Mk-82 and the Mk-122 Fireye. (After we shoot up all the fancy and expensive stuff during the first few hours of the war this is what we will have left.)

Mk-82

The Mk-82 is a 500lb general-purpose bomb that is effective against all above-ground structures including radar sites and bridges. In the simulation, just as in the real world, you can drop this baby on just about any enemy target and turn it into scrap metal.

Mk-122 Fireye

This weapon is more commonly called finned napalm. It is no longer used in the real world but I have to admit I sure enjoy using it in the simulation. Napalm consists of a highly flammable gel that hits the ground and ignites, creating a wall of fire. It is effective against all above-ground structures except bridges.

Low-Drag Symbology

The F-19 has three low-drag bomb aiming cues. This first two are the aiming diamond and range bar used for dropping high-drag bombs. The third one is called the Continuously Computing Impact Point (CCIP) pipper. This pipper (or aiming cue) consists of a line extending down from the HUD Flight Path Marker. At the end of this line is a circle with a dot in the middle that indicates the bomb impact point (or where the bomb will hit if the pilot releases it at that moment). When the dot in the middle gets

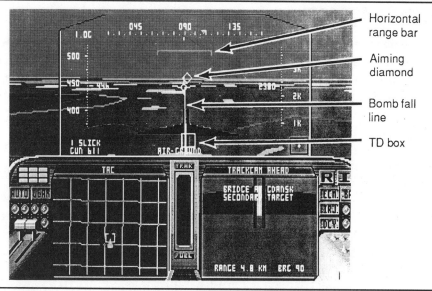

Horizontal
range bar

Aiming
diamond

Bomb fall
line

TD box

Figure 4-12. Low-Drag Bomb Symbology

to the target, the pilot pickles (releases) the bomb and hits the target. Figure 4-12 shows the low-drag bomb aiming symbology.

AIR-TO-AIR WEAPONS

The F-19 is armed with three types of air-to-air armament. The first type is a radar-guided AIM-120 AMRAAM. The second is the heat-seeking AIM-9 Sidewinder missile. The last, and one of the most effective F-19 air-to-air weapons, is the 20-mm Cannon. These weapons make the Stealth Fighter a deadly air combat adversary. We will discuss tactical employment of these weapons in the next chapter. In this section we will cover the capabilities of these weapons and the associated HUD symbology.

Air-to-Air Sensors

The air-to-air sensors used in the F-19 to detect and engage air targets are the same as the sensors used for ground attack. The left MFD Tactical (Tac) Display shows a God's eye view of the battle and is the best way to find and attack enemy aircraft. To enter the Tac Display press the F3 key until the word "Tac" appears at the top of the right MFD. Figure 4-13 shows the Tac Display depicting an enemy aircraft. On the right MFD the FLIR/Optics sensor will lock-on and display the range and bearing of the first target that it encounters. If you place the HUD in the air-to-air mode by hitting the F2 key until the words "AIR-AIR" appear in the bottom of the HUD, the FLIR/Optics sensor will only lock-on to aircraft targets. With the HUD in the air-to-ground mode the sensor locks on to ground targets, and with the HUD in the "Nav" mode it only locks on to runways. Figure 4-14 shows an aircraft displayed in the right MFD. Notice that the aircraft type and the bearing and range to the target are all displayed in the MFD.

A Target Designator (TD) box will appear in the HUD around the target that is being tracked and displayed by the FLIR/Optics sensor just

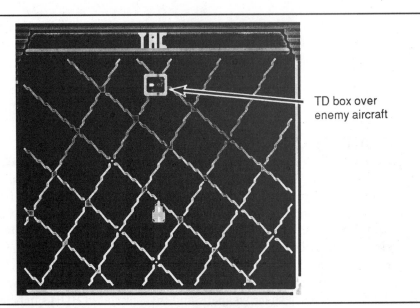

TD box over enemy aircraft

Figure 4-13. Enemy aircraft in the Tac Display

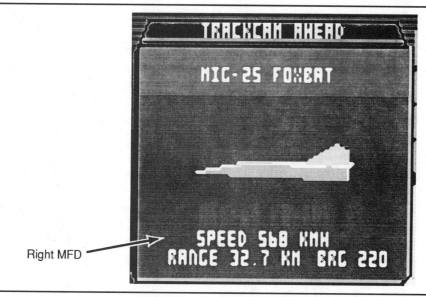

Right MFD

Figure 4-14.   FLIR/Optics Sensor locked on to MiG

as in the air-to-ground mode. You can command the sensor to search for a new target in the same way that you do in the air-to-ground mode. Pressing the **B** key will command the FLIR/Optics sensor to search its field of view (FOV) for a new target.

AIM-120 AMRAAM

The AIM-120 shown here

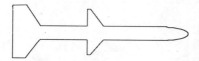

is a radar-guided missile with an active seeker head. Most of the early radar missiles such as the Aim-7 Sparrow were semi-active. What this means is that they guided on reflected radar energy. The launching aircraft had to keep a radar lock-on to the target in order for the missile to guide.

The Advanced Medium Range Air-to-Air Missile (AMRAAM) has its own radar that tracks the target and provides guidance for the missile, making it a true launch and leave weapon. The right MFD gives the pilot the same "shoot stupid" cue in air-to-air as it has in air-to-ground. A cross will appear over the target in the right MFD and the words "Missile Lock" will appear on the display. Figure 4-15 shows this display.

The pilot selects the AMRAAM by first entering the air-to-air HUD mode (hitting the F2 key) and then pressing the SPACEBAR until "AIM-120" appears in the lower-left corner of the HUD. The HUD display for the AMRAAM (and the Sidewinder) features a large circle in the middle of the HUD that shows the missile seeker head field of view (FOV). The target must be within this circle in order for the missile to lock-on to the target. Figure 4-15 also shows the HUD symbology for the AMRAAM.

The AMRAAM is the F-19 pilot's long lance and can be fired out to 32 kilometers. This long range allows you to go head to head with the advanced enemy fighters such as the MiG-29 and the Su-27 and have a *first shot opportunity*.

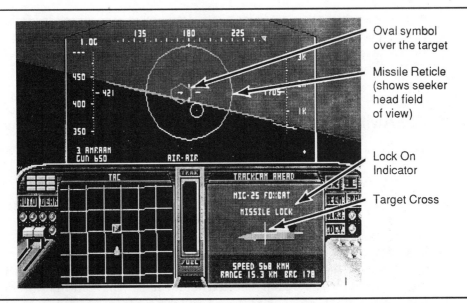

Oval symbol over the target

Missile Reticle (shows seeker head field of view)

Lock On Indicator

Target Cross

Figure 4-15. AMRAAM Symbology

Aim-9 Sidewinder

The Sidewinder, shown here

has identical HUD symbology as the AMRAAM. There are only two small differences between the two missiles in the F-19 simulation. The first is range. The AMRAAM is a slightly bigger missile and uses advanced rocket motor technology to give it longer legs.

The second difference is that the Sidewinder has a smaller field of view than the AMRAAM. The field of view of the missile is represented by the size of the Missile Reticle in the HUD. Figure 4-16 shows the HUD symbology for the Sidewinder—notice that it is slightly smaller than the AMRAAM Reticle. The Sidewinder is a heat-seeking missile that can be used in the F-19 simulation at shorter ranges than the AMRAAM. How-

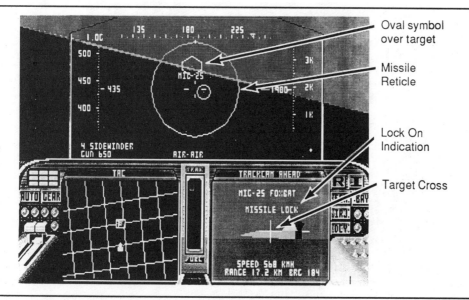

Figure 4-16. Sidewinder Symbology

ever, aiming and firing is identical for both missiles as are the keyboard controls and sensor displays.

The 20-mm Cannon

The 20-mm Cannon, also referred to as "the gun," is by far the most important air-to-air weapon in the F-19. The gun is very effective at close ranges and can be used from all target aspects. The F-19 carries 650 rounds of ammunition, and the number of rounds remaining is displayed in the lower-left corner of the HUD. Figure 4-17 shows the gun HUD symbology. The primary aiming reference for the gun is the fixed Gun Cross at the top of the HUD. The other aiming device for the gun is the Gun Reticle. This reticle is a historic gun sight, which means that it is very difficult to use and not the best gun aiming reference.

Gun shots in fighters require the fighter pilot to predict a future event. This event is the position of the target one bullet time of flight from

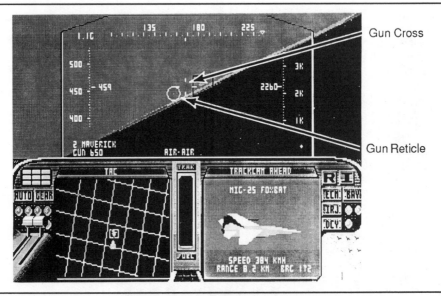

Figure 4-17.   Air-to-Air Gun Symbology

the firing. Gun aiming theory is very complex and involves some intricate math. Fortunately for you, I slept through this class at the Weapons School so I don't really understand gun aiming theory from a mathematical perspective. I do know that a historical sight like the snapshoot line in the F-16 or the Gun Aiming Reticle in the F-19 simulation are difficult to use because what you really need to aim the gun is predictive in nature, not historic. You don't care where the bullets would have gone if you had been firing. What you really need to know is where to put the jet to get the bullets to hit the target .5 to 1.5 seconds from when you fire (the average amount of time it takes for a bullet to travel from your jet to the target). In the next chapter, I will explain how to use the aiming references available in the F-19 to gun MiGs.

WEAPONS WRAP-UP

A fighter pilot must know his weapons. The F-19 features every bomb and missile in the U.S. inventory and adds a few more for good measure. This gives the F-19 pilot the maximum amount of flexibility when choosing weapons for a mission but requires the pilot to possess a great deal of academic knowledge. I strongly recommend that you acquire experience in a few favorites until you become good at using them rather than flying with a different weapons configuration each time you fly. As you gain experience you can add weapons to your personal weapons inventory.

The rest of the book will deal with fighting in the F-19. It is finally time to teach our enemies that if you mess with the bull you get the horn.

5

Air Combat Maneuvering

"The fighter pilot, even when handling a defensive task, must never lose the initiative to his opponent."
Adolf Galland,
WWII Luftwaffe Ace

Our flight of four F-4s had just come off the tanker and we were headed east toward the coast on the way to the target area on my first Cope Thunder mission. Cope Thunder is a two-week exercise held in the Philippines, where fighters come from all over the Pacific to participate in a large-scale simulated air war. This war encompasses both air-to-air and air-to-ground sorties. My squadron, the 90th Tactical Fighter Squadron, was tasked to fly defense suppression (Wild Weasel) missions, which entailed locating and attacking SAM sites. The squadron had just recently converted from the air-to-air to the Wild Weasel role and 12 of our 24 F-4Es had been replaced with 12 F-4Gs. The F-4G has a special threat warning system called the APR-38 that can locate and plot enemy radar sites. On this mission, each F-4 was carrying six Mk-82 500lb bombs to drop on the radar sites once we had located them.

The tanker track was located 100 miles feet wet (out to sea) and as we descended out of the track and started to accelerate, my heart started to beat faster. The 90th was my first fighter squadron; this was my first important mission as a combat-ready fighter pilot. I kept repeating the fighter pilot prayer as the airspeed increased and the Philippine coastline appeared on the horizon: "please God, don't let me screw this up." The flight lead on this mission was a great fighter pilot named Monroe. Monroe was our squadron Weapons and Tactics Officer and was well known in the Pacific for his prowess and audacity. I was flying as his wingman in the number two position.

As the airspeed approached 480 knots Monroe called for the flight to go into a battle box formation. In this formation, the front *element* (an element is two aircraft) flies line abreast one mile apart. The trailing element is between 1.5 to 2 miles back from the first element with the same one mile spread between the aircraft. This formation looks like a box when viewed from the top.

Just as I started to move out to the line abreast position I was stunned to see the bombs fall off of Monroe's jet. I couldn't figure out what was going on. My leader was dropping his bombs 50 miles from the coastline into the empty ocean. I couldn't remember him saying anything about this in the briefing so I hesitated for about half a second and then reached down, armed up my bombs, and pickled them off into the ocean. I didn't know if this was a planned maneuver or not, but if it was, I didn't want to be the cone head with 3,000 pounds of bombs stuck on his jet. After the bombs came off my aircraft, Monroe came on the radio and said, "You really didn't think we were going to haul those bombs all the way into the target area, did you Pete?" It seems that everyone but me knew about Monroe's plan to jettison our bombs into the ocean. They just wanted to see how the new Lieutenant would react. I passed the test.

It soon became apparent why we had lightened our load as the radar scope filled with bandits. F-5 Aggressor aircraft were being vectored on our flight by the enemy Ground Control Intercept (GCI). We were the first flight to push off toward the target, so we were going to bear the brunt of the enemy air defenses. On this mission we could not use our long-range Sparrow missiles unless we visually identified the enemy. This normally occurs inside 3 miles on a F-5 sized target, which is inside of minimum Sparrow range. This is exactly what happened in this fight as both sides came together at over 2,000 mph.

Monroe was the first to spot the F-5s, and he immediately started a pull up into a brown-colored bandit that was nose on to our element, eleven o'clock high. I was on Monroe's right side and collapsed to trail formation as he started a 7*G* turn to get behind the bandit. I kept pulling hard to stay with Monroe when my back seater called me to break right for another F-5 that was entering the fight from the south. I told Monroe that I was *stripped* (pulled out of formation) and that he was on his own. I passed this F-5 head to head, and kept pulling hard nose low to get behind him. The radio was filled with chatter as a mature turning engagement developed between Phantoms and F-5s.

Over in my corner of the war, things were looking bad for the home team. I had entered a level "let's see who can out turn each other" fight with the F-5 and it was rapidly becoming apparent that he had the better jet for a level nose pointing contest. We started on opposite ends of a circle that kept getting smaller. As this occurred, the F-5 was moving around the circle toward my six o'clock. There was nothing I could do to improve my position. I was stuck. In another minute the F-5 would get behind me and gun my brains out. The fact that this was simulated combat didn't make me any less disgusted with the situation.

As I got ready to start my last ditch guns defense maneuver, I heard Monroe's Texas drawl come over the radio: "How about I come on down there and give you a little help kid; looks like you've been treed by a chihuahua." Before I could answer, Monroe's Phantom slid effortlessly behind my assailant, and it was the F-5 who ended up doing the last ditch guns defense. Monroe had already killed the first F-5 we'd seen and had been hawking my fight from above. As the situation deteriorated he came in to save me. After "killing" the F-5, Monroe called for a separation and we bugged out of the fight.

Later, back in the squadron, Monroe and I debriefed the mission. I explained to him the starting conditions of my fight with the F-5 and how it developed into a flat *luftberry* (a luftberry is two aircraft on opposite ends of a circle pulling toward each other to get an advantage). After I described the fight Monroe stated, "Pete, you will one day be a great air-to-air fighter pilot." Wow, Monroe himself said that I would be great. However, before I could bask in the glow he continued, "*if* you do all of your air-to-air flying in a MiG-17." The MiG-17 is the best turning aircraft in the world in a flat nose pointing fight. Even today's modern fighters such as the F-16 and F-18 would have their hands full fighting a MiG-17 in a horizontal turning fight. "You will never be any good in an F-4 or anything else the Air Force flies if you don't learn to use the vertical." We went back to the start of the fight and he explained to me how I should have maneuvered the jet using both the horizontal and the vertical.

This was the first mission that I flew with Monroe; over the next year he taught me how to fight air-to-air with the Phantom. He used to say, "Pete, when it comes to flying fighters, you meet a better class of people in the vertical." Although Monroe is no longer with us, his tactical perspective lives on in the fighter pilots that he instructed. I will pass some of these lessons on to you in this and the following chapters of this book.

BASIC FIGHTER MANEUVERS

Basic Fighter Maneuvers, or BFM as it is most commonly called, is the foundation of all fighter missions. Maneuvering a jet in relation to the ground or another jet is the core skill in a fighter pilot's bag of tricks. You must be able to perform one-on-one BFM with an opposing aircraft or you will never be able to handle more advanced one-versus-many scenarios. BFM is broken down into three parts: offense, defense, and head-on maneuvering. Successful F-19 pilots must understand these concepts thoroughly in order to achieve their full potential in the simulation.

Energy for Position

When you maneuver a fighter you exchange energy for position. Energy, for the purpose of our discussion, is fighter speed and altitude. When fighting another aircraft and executing BFM you pull Gs to gain an advantage or defend yourself. You already have learned in Chapter 3 how fast you give up airspeed and altitude when pulling Gs in the F-19 simulation. It is very important to learn BFM in the F-19 because the less energy you have to start with, the more efficient you need to be when exchanging it for position. This discussion will help you use the limited energy of the F-19 to maneuver effectively against the enemy.

BFM is Flown in the Future

It has been said that with enough bananas you could teach a monkey to fly. I believe this statement is true. There is not enough bananas in the world, however, to teach a monkey to fly BFM. BFM consists of analyzing a dynamic three-dimensional problem in fractions of a second. This process does not take place in the safe, slow-paced 1G world that exists on the ground. Rather it occurs in the dangerous world of high tempo air combat. In this environment, in-depth analysis is a luxury that the fighter pilot cannot afford. The following are basic steps that must be rapidly executed by the fighter pilot when flying BFM:

1. *Observe* the bandit.

2. *Predict* the future of the bandit based upon your present observation of the bandit.

3. *Maneuver* the jet in response to this prediction.

4. *React* to changes in situation as you maneuver.

It is clear from this list that a large part of flying BFM is predicting the future position of the bandit. As we continue our discussion of BFM, remember that you must fly your jet in relation to where the bandit is going, not where he is when you observe him.

BFM GEOMETRY

In order to fly BFM, the pilot must understand the spatial relationship to the target from four perspectives: positional geometry, attack geometry, the weapons envelope, and the control zone.

Positional Geometry

Range, aspect angle, and *angle-off* are depicted in Figure 5-1, which shows the *positional geometry*—the geometric relationship between two aircraft. This relationship in turn defines the position advantage or disadvantage of one fighter to another.

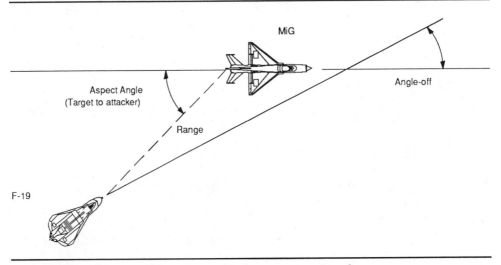

Figure 5-1. Angular relationship between two aircraft

Range   This is the distance between your jet and the bandit.

Aspect Angle   This is the number of degrees measured from the tail of the target to your aircraft. Aspect angle is important because it tells you how far away you are in degrees from the six o'clock position of the bandit.

Angle-off   This is the difference, measured in degrees, between your heading and the bandit's heading. This angle tells your relative fuselage alignment. For example, if the angle-off were 0 degrees you would be on a parallel heading with the bandit with your fuselages aligned. If the angle-off were 90 degrees, your fuselage would be perpendicular to that of the bandit.

Attack Geometry

Attack geometry describes the path that an offensive fighter takes when closing on the bandit. When you start an attack, there are three distinct paths or pursuit courses that you can follow. These are pure pursuit, lag pursuit, and lead pursuit. If you are pointing directly at the bandit you are flying a pure pursuit course. If you are pointing behind the bandit you are flying a lag pursuit course, and if you are pointing out in front of the bandit, you are flying lead pursuit. Figure 5-2 shows these different pursuit options. You can tell in F-19 which pursuit course you are flying by looking at your Gun Cross in relation to the bandit. Figure 5-3 shows an F-19 HUD with the Gun Cross out in front of the bandit. This is a lead pursuit course. If the Gun Cross were on the bandit you would be flying a pure pursuit course. If the Gun Cross were placed behind the bandit you would be flying lag pursuit.

The Weapons Envelope

The *weapons envelope* is the area around the bandit from which you can fire missiles or guns at the bandit. These parameters are defined by range, aspect angle, and angle-off. The dimensions and position of this area are dictated by the type of weapons that you are carrying.

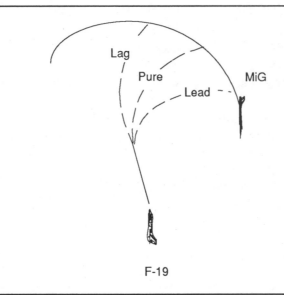

F-19

Figure 5-2. Pursuit options

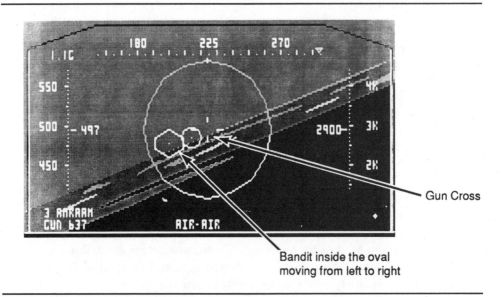

Gun Cross

Bandit inside the oval
moving from left to right

Figure 5-3. HUD view of lead pursuit

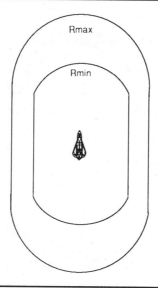

Figure 5-4. AMRAAM envelope

In the F-19 simulation, all the air-to-air missiles are all-aspect weapons. This means that you can fire them from all around the bandit. The only parameter that you need to watch is range. The shaded area in Figure 5-4 shows the weapons envelope of both the AIM-120 AMRAAM and the Sidewinder. The AIM-9 Sidewinder's envelope looks virtually identical with the exception of Rmax and Rmin, where $Rmax$ is maximum range and $Rmin$ is minimum range of the missile. The AMRAAM is a longer range missile, so both Rmax and Rmin are farther out on this missile than they are on a Sidewinder. This means you can shoot the AMRAAM at greater range from the target than the Sidewinder but the Sidewinder can be fired closer to the target than the AMRAAM. Figure 5-5 shows the weapons envelope of the AIM-9 Sidewinder.

The Control Zone

The *control zone,* also called the *elbow,* is the area behind the bandit where you can establish a stable position in which to employ weapons. From this

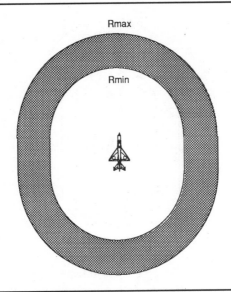

Figure 5-5. Sidewinder envelope

position it is relatively easy to remain behind the bandit and in control. (This spot is called the elbow because when fighter pilots describe air combat with their hands, the elbow of the arm that is showing the bandit's motion is the approximate position of the control zone.)

In the F-19 you face a wide variety of enemy aircraft but the control zone is virtually the same place for every jet you fight. If the enemy is at high airspeed, the control zone is between 3,000-4,000 feet at the bandit's six o'clock. As the bandit turns and expends energy, the aircraft's turn rate goes down (the bandit loses the ability to move the jet's nose) so you can move in closer and still have control. The control position will then move in as the bandit slows down. Along with range, the control position is also defined by angle-off and aspect. To be in the control zone you must be within 30 degrees of the target's tail with the angle-off less than 30 degrees. Figure 5-6 shows the control position as a cone at the six o'clock position of the bandit.

If all this elbow stuff sounds confusing to you, take heart. It really just amounts to flying around behind the bandit. We are just discussing terms so you will understand the description of the air-to-air battle in the

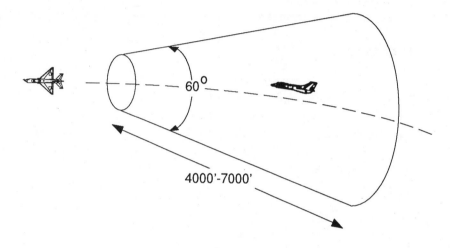

Figure 5-6.   The control position

next few sections. Just remember that air combat is not a process of in-depth analysis, and nobody ever accused a fighter pilot of being intellectual. If you are slightly befuddled then you are in the right frame of mind to fight air combat.

For now we will continue with our definition of terms.

BFM MECHANICS

An aircraft can do three things: roll, turn, and accelerate. Roll is used to position your lift vector. The nose of the jet will turn in the direction of your lift vector once you put *G*s on the aircraft. Offensive BFM involves turning your jet to solve aspect, angle-off, and overtake problems caused by the bandit's turns. Unfortunately, this is not an easy task. You must know precisely where and how to turn in order to successfully solve these problems and remain behind the bandit. To learn this, we will discuss the characteristics of a turning jet.

Turn Rate and Radius

Two characteristics of a turning aircraft that a fighter pilot must understand are turn radius and rate. *Turn radius* is simply a measure of how tightly your jet is turning. If you were looking down on the aircraft as it turned, turn radius would be the distance from the center of your turn circle to the aircraft, measured in feet. Figure 5-7 shows this circle.

The equation for turn radius is:

$$\text{Turn radius} = \frac{V^2}{gG}$$

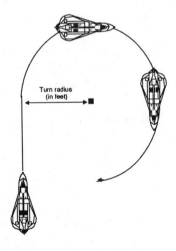

Turn radius
(in feet)

Figure 5-7. Aircraft turn circle

V is the aircraft's velocity in feet per second. Little *g* is gravity and big *G* is the *G*s the aircraft is pulling.

It is not important that you understand how to compute turn radius but it is important that you realize that velocity is squared in the turn radius equation. This means the fighter pilot must control his velocity (airspeed) to control his turn radius. The equation also includes aircraft *G*s. The more *G*s that you pull, the tighter the turn.

Turn rate is the second important characteristic of turning the jet. *Turn rate* is how fast the aircraft is moving around the turn circle we just talked about, or how fast an aircraft can move its nose. Turn rate is measured in degrees per second and is also dependent on *G*s and airspeed.

The equation for turn rate is:

$$\text{Turn rate} = \frac{KG}{V}$$

K is a constant and *G* and *V* are, again, the *G*s the aircraft is pulling and velocity. This equation tells the fighter pilot that commanding the highest *G*s possible, at the slowest airspeed, yields the best turn rate. Turn rate is very important in BFM because it is a measure of how fast you can put your nose on the bandit. Since you have to get your nose on an enemy aircraft to get a shot, it is obviously an advantage to have a high turn rate.

Acceleration

Acceleration is how fast you go faster. Since the F-19 bleeds off so much airspeed under *G,* and airspeed is what you need to generate turn rate, how well you get back this airspeed is very important. To accelerate in the F-19 you must *roll the wings level and be at full power!* If you do not roll the wings level you will still be under *G* and will not gain back any knots. You must also be at full power because the jet is such a pig that it will not accelerate well even at full power, much less at the lower thrust settings. Another thing that helps you accelerate is little *g*. To use little *g* (or gravity as it is more commonly called) get the nose of the jet below the horizon.

F-19 OFFENSIVE BFM

We have covered the geometry of fight and some basic terms. It is now time to discuss specific offensive, defensive, and head-on F-19 BFM. In an air-to-air fight, the bandit will turn in an attempt to kill you. The bandit's maneuvers will cause you aspect, angle-off, and range problems that must be solved by proper BFM. The goal here is to ensure that the bandit is the one that has a chance to test the ejection seat.

In any air-to-air fight you react to the bandit based on what you observe him doing. In the F-19 simulation you obviously don't have a pilot's out-the-canopy view. Instead, you are restricted to a computer monitor view of the battle, which makes visual air-to-air combat a real challenge. Fortunately, the F-19 has an excellent Tactical Display to augment the pilot's HUD view of the air battle. With the HUD and the Tactical Display you can easily execute all of the BFM you will need in the F-19.

Flying to the Elbow

Offensive Basic Fighter Maneuvers are flown when you are behind the bandit's 3/9 line. Figure 5-8 shows the F-19 with the 3/9 line drawn. This

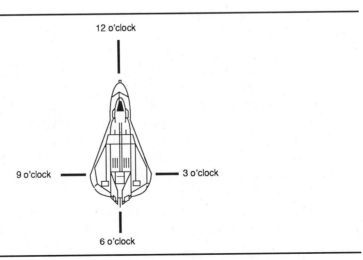

Figure 5-8. F-19 3/9 line

is simply a line drawn from the three o'clock to the nine o'clock position. If you are behind this line and between 1 to 3 miles (about 1.5 to 5 kilometers) you are in a position to fly offensive BFM. We will cover what to do when the bandit is outside of this range later in the book. If you are within 1 to 3 miles of the bandit but not behind the 3/9 line then you should fly head-on or defensive BFM. We will cover both of these next. For now we will concentrate on the proper maneuvers to use to stay behind a turning bandit. We have already discussed why you want to get to the bandit's elbow but it is worth repeating. From the elbow you can easily stay established behind the bandit and in a position to shoot.

What makes offensive BFM difficult is the bandit's turn. The harder the bandit turns, the more aspect and angle-off problems are created for the attacker. When the bandit turns, you have to solve these problems with a turn of your own. The following procedures will discuss how and when to turn to arrive and stay at the bandit's elbow.

The first thing you need to accomplish to fly BFM is to choose the right weapons and bring up the proper displays. In the F-19 you should call up the air-to-air mode of the HUD by hitting the F2 key until AIR-AIR appears at the bottom of the HUD. Next, press the SPACEBAR to select your air-to-air missiles. If you have both AIM-120s and AIM-9s loaded, call up your AIM-9s because they are more effective at close range. Next, call up the Tactical Display on the left MFD by pressing F3 until it appears. Finally, you should strive to get your FLIR/Optics sensor locked on to the target that you are fighting. This will automatically lock-on your missiles and give you a TD box in the HUD around the target. To achieve this lock, press the / key and observe which aircraft is locked up by the sensor. If it is the wrong one, hit the **B** key until you get a TD box in the HUD around the correct aircraft. Remember you can also use the Tactical Display to check your lock-on.

You are now ready to fly offensive BFM.

1. The first step is to *observe* the Tactical Display to see which way the bandit is turning. You can easily note the bandit's direction of turn on the Tactical Display.

If the bandit is not turning then you don't need to worry about flying offensive BFM. Go to full power to close the range and shoot as soon as you get a "shoot stupid cue." To paraphrase an old crook, "let me make one thing perfectly clear"—the object of offensive BFM is not to just fly around behind the bandit. The object of offensive BFM is to fill the bandit's cockpit with hair, teeth, and eyeballs as quickly as possible. You need to know how to fly offensive BFM in case your missiles go stupid or you are out of missiles. When this happens you have to get to the elbow to keep control of the bandit and get a gun shoot.

2. After observing the bandit's direction of turn, *predict* his movement across the sky and start a turn in the same direction. Go to full power by pressing the SHIFT key and hitting the + key.

3. As the bandit starts turning out in front of you, *maneuver* to place the Gun Cross out in front of the MiG (lead pursuit) and roll the wings up to 70-80 degrees of bank to pull 5Gs to 7Gs. Figure 5-9 shows this position on the bandit.

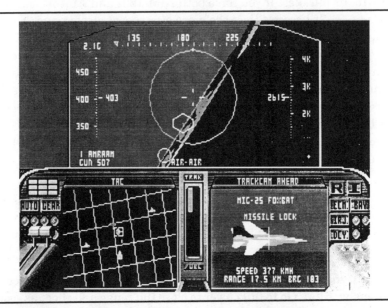

Figure 5-9.   Lead pursuit course

4. You now *observe* the bandit's movement in your HUD to determine how you will *react*.

   The bandit will do one of three things in relation to the Flight Path Marker in your HUD:

- If he stays in the same spot in the HUD, you are matching the bandit's turn rate and will close the range and fly to the elbow. Just keep everything the same and you will soon be in range for a gun shot. When you can see the details of the bandit such as the wings and the tail you are in range for a gun shot.

- If you pull the Gun Cross to lead and the bandit moves rapidly across your HUD and back under your nose, ease off the *G*s by rolling out of some of your bank and let the bandit fly back into view. In this case you are pulling too much lead for the bandit's present turn rate. Once you regain a tally ho, put the Gun Cross behind the bandit and fly a lag pursuit course. Figure 5-10 shows a HUD view of lagging the bandit. As you get closer in lag pursuit the bandit will

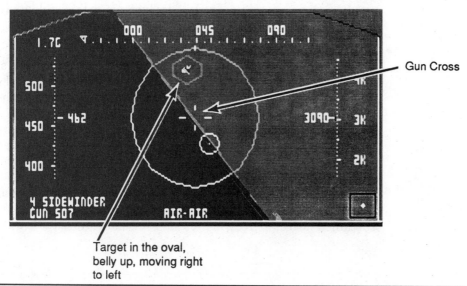

Target in the oval,
belly up, moving right
to left

Figure 5-10.   Lag pursuit course

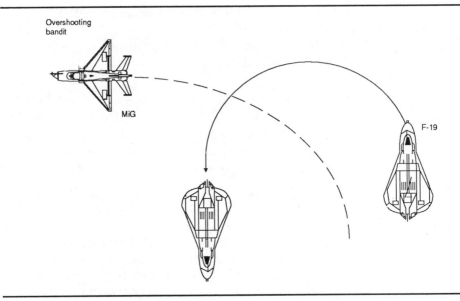

Figure 5-11. Bandit overshoot

start moving away from you in the direction of the turn. When this occurs, pull your nose back to lead by increasing the bank angle of the F-19. You should now be at the elbow in position for a gun shot.

- If the bandit moves through the Gun Cross and you are forced from lead to lag pursuit, you are not matching the bandit's turn rate and will *overshoot*. An overshoot is when you fly past the bandit and get spit out in front of his 3/9 line. Figure 5-11 shows an overshoot situation. This situation is not good since you are in danger of being transformed from the shooter to the shootee. To avoid this situation you must turn the jet harder by rolling into 80-90 degrees of bank. Remember that the F-19 automatically gives you Gs as a function of bank angle. If this doesn't work to stop the overshoot, keep the turn coming in the direction of the bandit and you should be able to get him back out front. Be careful not to stall the aircraft. A sustained turn at high Gs in the F-19 almost always leads to a stall.

When you see this occurring, roll some bank out and get the nose down to get some smash back.

These steps are designed to establish you at the elbow of the bandit. This is not a static situation. You will need to constantly maneuver the jet to gain and maintain this position. You will undoubtedly fall out of this position from time to time once you are in it. It is hard for many pilots to get used to the fluid, high tempo pace of an air-to-air battle. Just picture a spot behind the bandit and keep striving to fly to this spot. On the way there shoot any time you get a chance. The easiest BFM you can fly is against a mass of flaming wreckage.

F-19 DEFENSIVE BFM

What if the bandit starts out behind your 3/9 line? There is not much creative thought that goes into defensive BFM. In fact, if you think about what you are going to do too much you will end up getting your rear end shredded by an enemy missile. The fundamental principle behind flying defensive BFM is to keep fighting. Don't give up or get lazy no matter how bleak the situation appears. The fight is not over until you are dead or in your chute.

Maneuver and Countermeasures

The first thing you need to do when you find yourself on the defensive is to create BFM problems for the bandit. You do this by rolling the jet up to 80-90 degrees of bank, pulling 7Gs to 8Gs, and giving him a face full of airplane. You already know how hard it is to stay behind a hard turning bandit so return the favor. The obvious difference in being on the defensive is that the bandit is the one who is in position to shoot so you must be very vigilant.

Missile Launch

If you see a missile fired on your Tactical Display you must immediately execute the following procedures:

1. Dispense flares and chaff by hitting the **1** and **2** keys respectively. Continue pressing these keys, and also hit the **3** and **4** keys to turn on your IR and Radar Jammer. Don't worry about which kind of missile is fired. It is better to react fast to a missile launch and not waste valuable time pondering missile guidance theory.

2. Next, accelerate to put the missile on the beam as fast as possible. The *beam* is your three or nine o'clock position. A missile has the most difficult time tracking your jet when you place it on the beam. If the missile was fired from the beam, you should accomplish step one and then check into and then away from the missile. All of this maneuvering should be done using the Tactical Display. You should see the missile guiding away from your jet on the display if your countermeasures fooled the missile.

3. The F-19 gives the pilot a missile warning sound if an enemy missile is about to pass in close proximity. If you hear this sound, you should immediately put max Gs on the jet by pulling back on the stick and simultaneously dispense chaff and flares. After the missile passes, roll out of the bank and get the nose down to regain some airspeed.

Bandit Behind Your 3/9 Line

When you look at your Tactical Display and see a bandit behind your 3/9 line inside of missile range, it is time to execute your defensive BFM moves.

1. The first step is to roll the aircraft up to 70-80 degrees of bank and turn at $7G$s to $8G$s in the direction of the shortest distance

toward the bandit. All of this defensive maneuvering should be done while looking at the Tactical Display. This serves two purposes. The first is that you can easily see the geometry of the fight, and the second is that you can quickly spot any missiles that are being fired at your jet.

2. Next, note the direction of bandit movement on your Tactical Display and react accordingly

These reactions will include the following:

• If the bandit is moving toward your twelve o'clock position then your defensive turn is working and you will soon pass the bandit head-on. At this point you may get a chance for a gun or missile shot, and you can punish the fool for having the audacity to even get close to your jet.

• If you turn and the bandit does not move toward your twelve o'clock position then you are not turning hard enough. In F-19 this can be caused by two things. The first is that you simply need to pull more Gs. The second is that you do not have enough airspeed to pull high Gs. You can easily fix the first problem but if you are out of knots then you are in deep kimchi.

Unfortunately there is little you can do to defend yourself against a bandit when you are out of airspeed. What you should do in this case is make the best defensive turn you can with the knots you have and use your countermeasures if the bandit fires a missile at you. Do not give up and commit maneuvering suicide by stalling yourself into the ground. Make the bandit kill you. I have been in this situation a number of times in the F-19 simulation and three different real fighters—slow, low, and out of ideas when a bandit just blundered out in front of me and I hosed him. You just have to be tough in this situation, because the only magic moves to spit the bandit out in front are done in Hollywood.

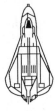

Figure 5-12.   Head on pass

F-19 HEAD-ON BFM

Head-on BFM is flown after passing the bandit nose to nose. Figure 5-12 shows a head-on pass. When passing a bandit in this situation you have two choices. The first is to blow through the fight and separate. The second choice is to turn and duke it out with the bandit. If you choose to duke it out then use the following head-on BFM procedures:

1. Shoot any time you can when approaching a bandit head-on. When you see the outline of the enemy's jet, you are usually too close for missiles so use the gun.

2. If the bandit shoots at you, disregard head-on BFM and fight the missile using the defensive procedures that we have already discussed.

3. If one of you doesn't get turned to hamburger before you pass head-on, then roll the jet toward the MiG and pull 7Gs to 8Gs to turn your nose on the bandit. Realize that the bandit is probably doing the same to get the MiG's nose on you.

4. Keep pulling until the MiG is in the HUD and then shoot. If you get the bandit in the HUD and you are behind the MiG's 3/9 line then you have out-turned your enemy and are now in control. If you are still in front of the MiG's 3/9 line then the bandit is matching your turn, and you must be alert for a missile shot on you. Keep pulling and shoot when you can.

Any time you are confused when flying offensive, defensive, or head-on BFM just turn in the direction of the bandit; get the bandit in the HUD and shoot. It is amazing how uncomplicated the fight gets when the sky is full of flaming bandits.

The AMRAAM and Sidewinder Missiles

The AMRAAM and Sidewinder are very easy missiles to use in the F-19 simulation. There are only three parameters that must be met to successfully launch either of these air-to-air missiles: maximum range (Rmax), minimum range (Rmin), and the Missile Aiming Reticle. We have already discussed the differences in these missiles. The AMRAAM can be fired from longer ranges but minimum range is also farther out. This makes it a relatively poor short-range weapon. The Sidewinder cannot be fired at long range but is still effective at shorter ranges. You can think of the AMRAAM as a long lance and the Sidewinder as a short sword. The pilot uses the same techniques for firing both of these missiles. These steps are used.

1. Select AIR-AIR in the HUD by hitting the F2 key until it appears in the bottom of the HUD.

2. Call up either a Sidewinder or an AMRAAM by pressing the SPACEBAR until the desired missile appears in the lower-left corner of the HUD.

3. Lock the FLIR/Optics Sensor on the correct target by pressing the / key and checking the target in the left MFD. A picture of the target that the sensor locks up to will appear in the left MFD. You should also have a TD box around the desired target in the HUD and the Tactical Display in the right MFD.

4. When a missile lock indication appears in the left MFD you are at Rmax and can shoot. Pull the target inside the Missile Reticle.

5. Note the target *line-of-sight rate.* This is how fast the target is moving across your HUD. If you cannot turn hard enough to keep the target in your HUD, for the next four seconds don't shoot—the target line-of-sight rate is too high. If you are trying to shoot an AMRAAM this time increases to six seconds.

6. When you do decide to shoot, open the bomb bay doors by pressing the **8** key.

7. Fire the missile with the number two fire button on your joystick or the ENTER key.

Again, there is a big difference between the AMRAAM and the Sidewinder in the F-19 simulation. If you have both missiles loaded, use the AMRAAM for the long-range shots and the Sidewinder for the close in maneuvering shots. If you only have one of them loaded, you can shoot anywhere inside of Rmax if you correctly judge the line-of-sight rate.

THE GUN

If the AMRAAM is your long lance and the Sidewinder is your short sword, then the gun can be considered a knife. The gun in the F-19 is the most lethal and satisfying air-to-air killing weapon. You start with 650 rounds of ammunition so you are virtually assured of having the gun available even at the end of the mission when you have fired or dropped everything else on the jet. The gun is most effective against close in maneuvering targets. Use the following steps to gun MiGs:

1. Select the gun by pressing the F2 key until "AIR-AIR" appears at the bottom of the HUD. Air-to-air guns are always available with or without a missile when called up in the air-to-air mode of the cockpit HUD.

2. Note the direction the target is moving, and fly to place the HUD Gun Cross out in front of the target. You must predict the target's path through the sky and place the Gun Cross in a spot where you predict the target will fly.

3. Open fire *before the target reaches the gun cross.* Remember, the name of the game here is a bullet-target rendezvous, and since your bullets have a .5 to 1.5 second flight time you must open fire early. You shoot the gun by pressing and holding the number one fire button on your joystick or by pressing and holding down the DEL key.

There are three different types of gun shots in air combat. These are the tracking gun shot, the high line-of-sight rate snapshot, and the low line-of-sight rate snapshot. The *tracking gun shot* is performed from the stabilized control position (the elbow) of the bandit, which we have already discussed in this chapter. This type of gun shot has the highest Pk (probability of kill) because you can remain in position and keep shooting. Bullet density is high and the conditions are stable.

The *high line-of-sight rate snapshot* is the opposite of the tracking gun shot. In this shot the target is moving quickly across the HUD. You must open fire early and way out in front of the bandit to hit the target. This shot occurs in head-on and beam situations or when the bandit is out-turning your jet.

The *low line-of-sight rate snapshot* occurs when you cannot quite turn hard enough to get in the control position. In this shot you must also open fire early but the target is not moving as fast across the HUD as in the high line-of-sight rate snapshot.

You can perform all of these gun shots using the simple steps outlined earlier. Just remember, when you see details of the bandit in the HUD (like wings and the fuselage) go to guns and shoot early.

THE BIG PICTURE

The F-19 Tactical Display gives the pilot a God's eye view of the air battle. This view is a fantastic aid in helping the fighter pilot understand what is happening in the fight. In real fighters you have to rely on your eyes and your radar, which do not give you as good a picture of the air battle as the Tactical Display. With this display you should be able to get the big picture of the fight and instantly see the results of your weapons launches and maneuvers. Remember that the object of air-to-air combat is to kill the enemy as quickly as possible—so use the Tac Display to size up the situation and then react accordingly. Later in the book, we will build from your basic BFM knowledge to put the entire air-to-air fight together.

6

GROUND ATTACK

"We loop in the purple twilight; We spin in the silvery dawn With black smoke trailing behind us; To show where our comrades have gone.
So stand to your glasses steady; This world is full of lies Here's a toast to those dead already; And here's to the next man to die."
From the fighter pilot song
Stand To Your Glasses

The klaxon sounded with an ear-splitting noise that was so loud you could feel it all the way through your body. Within seconds two F-4 Phantoms came to life in a cloud of black smoke, and crawled forward out of their concrete revetments, straining under eight tons of bombs. They moved down the taxiway straight toward the active runway and paused while ground crews pulled the arming pins on their weapons. This task accomplished in seconds, the Phantoms lumbered onto the runway. The lead jet immediately went to afterburner. A bright red flame as long as the aircraft shot out from behind the jet, pushing it forward. At the half-mile point down the long runway at Cam Ran Bay, the Phantom began to rotate for takeoff. The afterburner on the second aircraft now ignited with a roar and it too started down the runway. Soon the Phantoms were airborne, and within seconds both had disappeared into the western sky leaving a black smoke trail to mark their path.

Violence was the only word to describe the view from Raven 11. Raven was a lone, single-engine O-1 prop aircraft with the job of flying over the jungle and calling in close air support missions for Army troops. It was late in the day when Raven received a desperate call on his Fox Mike radio from an Army Infantry Company. It seemed that Bravo Company had run into what at first appeared to be a small enemy force. It soon became apparent that this small force was really a Regiment of North Vietnamese Regulars. The situation quickly turned desperate and Bravo Company, outnumbered three to one, was pushed back onto a small hill for what was starting to look like a last stand.

Raven 11 had been circling above the fight for an hour, and had called in two other air strikes that had done little to turn the tide of battle. Because of the close proximity of the friendlies to the bad guys, Raven was having trouble getting the close air support close enough to do any good. All attempts at getting the Company off the hill had failed—one Huey helicopter had already been shot down and three others damaged in the attempt. Night was descending on the jungle at an alarming rate and in another hour the battle would be blanketed in darkness. With night came the certainty of death and defeat for the Bravo Company.

Gunfighter 61 flight had been sitting CAS alert at Cam Ran Bay for only 10 minutes when the Klaxon went off. The scramble went smooth, and they were over the battle talking to Raven only 15 minutes after takeoff. Gunfighter lead was a wiry, mean-spirited major they called Snake. He was on his second tour in Southeast Asia, and had flown 100 missions "downtown" (into Hanoi and Haiphong) on his first tour in the F-105. Snake was not the kind of man you wanted as an enemy, circling above your head with napalm. His wingman was a new lieutenant they called Pig Pen because no matter how hard he tried he always looked like he'd just finished changing the oil in his car. Pig Pen had only been in country for two months, but like most other fighter pilots, he would do anything for a dime and give you a nickel change.

The Phantoms set up an orbit to the east of the battle to receive a quick briefing from Raven. The situation was now so desperate that when Raven asked the Army commander how close the enemy was to their position, he answered, "If I hold the mike out in front of me you can talk to them." As Raven spoke to Gunfighter, the Fox Mike radio came alive with the sounds of battle. The enemy had broken through the perimeter and was massing troops at this location. An army lieutenant acting as the company commander was calling for an immediate air strike and had waived all the rules on proximity to friendlies. It was now or never for Bravo Company.

Raven rolled in and fired a smoke rocket at the side of the hill that was being overrun. As he pulled off and looked down he saw the earth crawling with North Vietnamese. "That's a good mark Gunfighter, hit my smoke," Raven called. "You're cleared in hot; the friendlies are on the high ground to the North."

Snake bent his jet around into a hard right turn and started a long dive toward the ground. The white phosphorous smoke from Raven's rocket was hard to see in the twilight but he did see the spot where it had flashed against the ground. The Phantom dove into the haze of the battle and Snake strained to pick up sight of the target area through the darkness and smoke. Just before he reached the point where he would have to pull the Phantom up out of the dive, hundreds of dark shapes appeared through the mist. Enemy soldiers filled the reticle of Snake's bomb sight and within an instant he pickled his bombs and was climbing away from the battle.

Some of the North Vietnamese saw the Phantom for a split second as four silver canisters fell from the aircraft and tumbled end over end toward the ground at their feet. Snake had caught the main body of North Vietnamese just as they were exposed and charging through open ground on the side of the hill. This area erupted into an inferno as the napalm detonated with a blinding flash of light. The troops that where caught in the open were the leading edge of the attacking wave, and they were killed immediately. The rest of the attack faltered and started to fall back down the mountain just as Pig Pen's bombs hit the same area with equally devasting results.

With a large number of enemy soldiers turned to toast on the side of the hill Raven could see that now was the time to try for an extraction. He got on the radio and reported the situation had stabilized temporarily. The Hueys were called in again and in a short time arrived and started to load troops. Gunfighter flight kept making repeated napalm and strafe passes to hold the North Vietnamese at bay and as darkness fell the last Huey lifted off the hill. The attack by Gunfighter had swayed the resolve of the enemy at a critical time in their attack, which allowed the helicopters to get in and out in the confusion. The Phantoms had run out of bombs and bullets long before the extraction was complete but continued to make "dry" passes over the enemy to keep their heads down. With the rescue of Bravo Company completed, the Gunfighters rejoined and headed east for home.

F-19 AIR-TO-GROUND FUNDAMENTALS

Attacking ground targets is a difficult and dangerous job. Most of the aircraft shot down in aerial combat have been lost while performing ground-attack missions. Ground-attack missions, however, are of critical importance as demonstrated in the battle described previously. In the F-19 simulation there are a number of ground-attack missions that form the core scenarios in the game. These missions are by far the most challenging and difficult part of the simulation and require the most skill and cunning. On air-to-air missions you fight air-to-air. On air-to-ground missions you not only drop bombs or shoot missiles at ground targets, you also fight air-to-air when you are threatened by enemy fighters. For this reason you must build a strong foundation in basic air-to-ground skills so that they will become second nature to you in the heat of battle.

Attacking ground targets is not that different from attacking aircraft. You must fly BFM to place your jet in a position to release your weapons at the target. The F-19 simulation has five different types of weapons that require unique attack profiles. These weapons are:

- 20-mm Cannon

- Air-to-Ground Missiles

- Low-Drag Bombs

- High-Drag Bombs (to include CBU types)

- Laser-Guided Bombs

This chapter will cover all of these weapons in detail along with the F-19 attack profiles used to release them. In addition, we will discuss the reconnaissance and aerial resupply missions.

The 20-mm Cannon

The F-19 20-mm cannon is primarily an air-to-air weapon. It can be used if necessary against fragile targets such as radars and SAM sites. Strafing ground targets is very simple in concept. You simply aim the Gun Cross in the HUD at the target and open fire. The bullets fly straight out the Gun Cross toward the target, and you can observe the tracers in the HUD and adjust your aimpoint. The following steps may improve your strafe success:

1. Call up the air-to-ground mode in the HUD by hitting the F2 key until "AIR-GROUND" appears in the bottom center of the HUD. Any time you are in this mode, the gun is hot and you can strafe no matter what other weapons are called up.

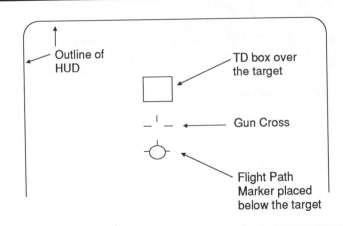

Figure 6-1. Initial Flight Path Marker placement for strafe

2. Once you gain sight of the target, place the Flight Path Marker in the HUD below the target (as shown in Figure 6-1). You do this to have a smooth and controlled approach. If you aim at the target with the Gun Cross without lining up, it is very easy to start chasing the target with the Gun Cross and spraying bullets everywhere but on the target.

3. Gradually move the Gun Cross up to the target and stabilize it. Be careful not to use too much bank if you have a small azimuth correction to make. Remember bank angles equates to G, and you will definitely be in for a wild ride if you bank too much to line up the shot.

4. Open fire by pressing and holding the number one fire button on your joystick or the BACKSPACE key on the keyboard. Shoot in one- to two-second bursts, and pause in between shots to observe the results and adjust your aimpoint if necessary.

5. It is very hard to detect ground rush at the low approach angle normally associated with strafe. For this reason, you must pull the jet up and away from the target before you detect the ground rising up to flatten you.

Strafing with 20-mm is not effective against hard targets such as bridges and bunkers, but for soft targets that just appear out in front of you it is an excellent pop-up weapon. You must be able to see the target visually in order to strafe it, and this is also a good gauge for shooting. When you can make out details on the target by looking through the HUD (you can tell that it is a radar site, for example) then the target is in range for a gun shot. There are no altitude or firing restrictions on a strafe pass. Be careful, however, of getting target fixation and double dribbling yourself off of the ground.

Air-to-Ground Missiles (AGMs)

The AGMs used by the F-19 are the Penguin, Harpoon, HARM, and the Maverick. Penguin and Harpoon are used for ship attack while the HARM is used against radars. Maverick is a general-purpose missile in the F-19 simulation, and it is effective against a variety of targets. All of these AGMs are "fire-and-forget" missiles that are aimed and released the same way by the F-19. Fire-and-forget missiles, as you will recall from Chapter 4, do not require pilot input after launch.

The following steps will give you a smooth attack sequence for AGM launch.

1. Call up the air-to-ground mode in the HUD by pressing the F2 key until "AIR-GROUND" appears at the bottom center of the HUD.

2. Call up the desired missile by hitting the SPACEBAR until the proper weapon name appears in the bottom-left corner of the HUD. Figure 6-2 shows the Maverick missile (AGM-65) called up in the HUD.

3. In the left MFD, bring up the FLIR/Optics sensor by hitting the / key. In the air-to-ground HUD mode this sensor will lock on to ground targets and will display them in the left MFD and provide you bearing and range to that target. If the target that appears in the MFD is not the correct target, press the **B** key to get the FLIR/Optics sensor to change targets. In Figure 6-2 you will notice that the words "Primary Target" appear on the display. This denotes that the sensor is locked on to the primary target. This sensor also tells the pilot when it is locked on to the

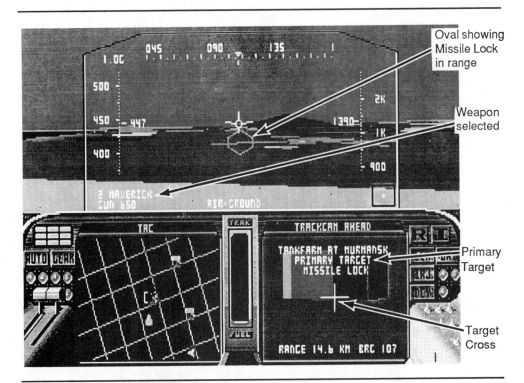

Figure 6-2. Air-to-Ground Missile (AGM) symbology—the Maverick missile called up in the HUD

secondary target. When the sensor locks to a target you also get a Target Designator box displayed in the HUD.

4. The missile will now lock on to the target automatically when it gets in range. A cross will appear in the MFD and the Target Designator Box in the HUD will change to an oval. You are now within Rmax (which is maximum range). This view is also shown in Figure 6-2.

Note: You can fire the missile anywhere inside Rmax but you will increase your probability of a hit if you wait for optimum range. A good rule of thumb for firing is to shoot as soon as you get inside Rmax any time you are being engaged by enemy aircraft or SAMs. If you are not being threatened by the enemy, wait until the target oval changes color to indicate that you are in optimum range.

5. In the F-19 simulation, you can fire all of the AGMs from any altitude above 500 feet. You should have no more than 30 degrees of bank at launch, and the target should be in the HUD. Try to place the target near the Gun Cross prior to shooting to ensure you are in the correct launch parameters. To fire, open the bomb bay doors by hitting the **8** key, and then press the number two fire button if you have a joystick or the ENTER key if you are using the keyboard.

6. After missile launch, close the bay doors by hitting the **8** key again. You can observe the missile fly out by pressing SHIFT-F4. This will allow you to ride the missile to impact. Do not use this feature unless the tactical environment is benign because while you are out riding the missile, you may get your aircraft shot out from underneath you. If you need to go back to the inside the cockpit view hit the F1 key.

All of these missiles are mechanized the same way in the F-19. Remember that when you get a missile lock on you, you are at Rmax and should wait and get closer before firing if the tactical situation allows.

Low-Drag Bombs

Low-drag bombs for the F-19 are the Mk-82 and the Mk-122. These bombs are not guided in any way and when they are pickled (released), they free-fall to the target. They are called low drag because after release they fall toward the target going almost the same speed as your aircraft. If you are too low at release this will cause a problem—the bomb will explode under your jet and turn some valuable parts of your body to Swiss cheese. Because the low-drag bomb is dumb (unguided) you must fly a precise path over the target in order to achieve accuracy. Both the Mk-82 and the Mk-122 are aimed and released in the same manner.

1. Call up the air-to-ground mode in the HUD by pressing the F2 key until "AIR-GROUND" appears at the bottom center of the HUD.

2. Call up the desired bomb by hitting the SPACEBAR until the proper weapon name appears in the bottom-left corner of the HUD. Figure 6-3 shows the Mk-82 (Slick) bomb called up in the HUD. Figure 6-3 also shows all of the aiming symbology associated with F-19 low-drag bombs. These consist of an Aiming Diamond to help you line up in azimuth, and a Range Bar at the top of the HUD. This bar gets smaller as the target approaches, and disappears entirely when you are at the proper bomb range.

The most important aiming reference for low-drag bombs is the CCIP (Continuously Computing Impact Point) pipper. This pipper consists of a dot surrounded by a small reticle attached to a line. The line is called the Bomb Fall Line, and it runs from the Flight Path Marker to the CCIP reticle. This line shows the future track of the reticle over the ground.

3. Lock the FLIR/Optics sensor on to the target by pressing the / key. You will get the same primary/secondary target confirmation in the left MFD on the target as you did with AGM missiles, but because you have free-fall bombs called up instead of missiles you will not get a missile lock indication.

4. Approach the target between 200-700 feet and line up your Flight Path Marker vertically with the diamond in your HUD. Figure 6-3 shows this diamond. At 18 kilometers start a 30-40 degree

climb to 7,500-8,500 feet. Open the bay doors by pressing the **8** key. At 5 kilometers out, push forward on the stick and start a dive toward the target by placing your Flight Path Marker slightly past the target as shown in Figure 6-4.

5. Ensure that the bomb fall line is through the target, and note the contraction of the Horizontal Ranging Cue at the top of the HUD. If you are not aligned in azimuth (left-right) on the target then make *small* corrections early in the bomb run to correct the problem.

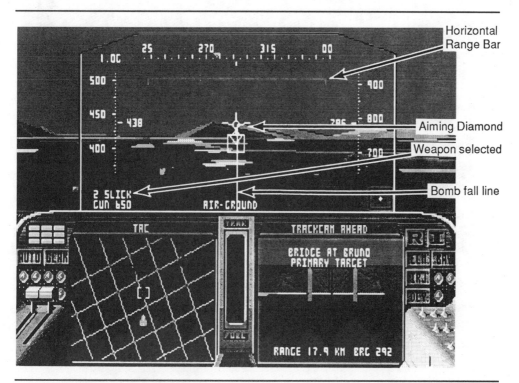

Figure 6-3.   Low-drag bomb symbology—the Mk-82 bomb called up in the HUD

6. Keep diving toward the target and when the CCIP pipper (specifically the dot in the center of the reticle) gets to the target, or the ranging bar shrinks to a single line, hit the number two fire button on the joystick or the ENTER key on the keyboard. Figure 6-5 shows the proper HUD picture of the target at pickle. It is very difficult to see the pipper on the target from the proper release altitude of 2,000-3,000 feet, so use the Ranging Bar as your primary reference. Always drop two bombs to ensure a hit. After you pickle, start a pull up away from the target to avoid flying through the fragmentation from the blast. As you climb away from the target, press the **8** key to close your bay doors.

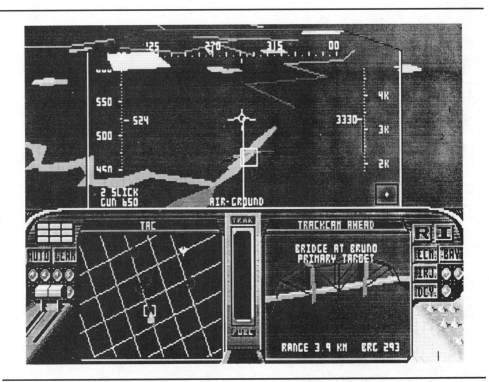

Figure 6-4.   Low-drag bomb pass

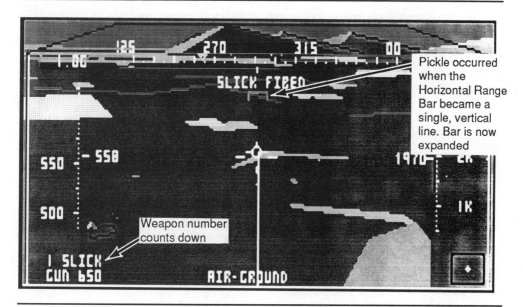

Figure 6-5. HUD view of Mk-82 Slick (low-drag bomb) at pickle

Low-drag bombs are more difficult than AGMs to employ because you have to fly directly over the target and line up your HUD aiming cues. In addition, you must be very careful not to get below 2,000 feet at release or you may *frag* yourself (fly through the blast). The HUD symbols will flash if you are danger of blowing yourself up with your own bombs. If you see the HUD symbols flash, go through dry (do not drop)!

High-Drag Bombs

The high-drag bombs used in the F-19 simulation are the Mk-20 Rockeye, the Durandal, the ISC B-1 minelets (CBUs), the Mk-82 Snakeye, and the Mk-35 IN cluster. These bombs are an odd assortment of real-world and F-19-specific weapons that use clam shells, parachutes, and fins. They all have one thing in common in the F-19 simulation: they are all aimed with

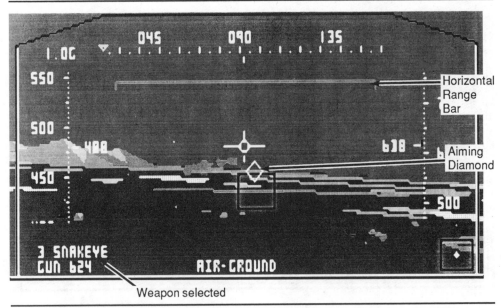

Figure 6-6.   High-drag bomb symbology—the Mk-82 called up in the HUD

the same high-drag aiming HUD aiming symbology. The following steps will help you place these high-drag bombs on the target:

1. Call up the air-to-ground mode and the desired bomb the same way you did for low-drag bombs. Hit the F2 key until "AIR-GROUND" appears at the bottom of the HUD and press the SPACEBAR until the proper weapon is showing in the lower-left corner of the HUD. Figure 6-6 shows the Mk-82 Snakeye called up in the HUD.

2. Lock the FLIR/Optics sensor on to the target by pressing the / key. Use the **B** key to find the proper target. Left MFD symbology is the same for low-drag and high-drag bombs. You will get a picture of the target displayed along with the bearing and range from your jet to the target. If the target is the primary or secondary target, this will also be shown on the left MFD.

3. Approach the target at 200-700 feet and at 8 kilometers start a shallow climb. Open the bay doors by pressing the **8** key and level off between 500-1,000 feet.

4. Line up the target by placing the Flight Path Marker on a vertical line with the Aiming Diamond in the HUD. Figure 6-7 shows these HUD high-drag bombing cues. The diamond is used to align your jet in azimuth with the target. The only other cue in the HUD for high-drag bombs is the Horizontal Ranging Bar, also shown in Figure 6-7.

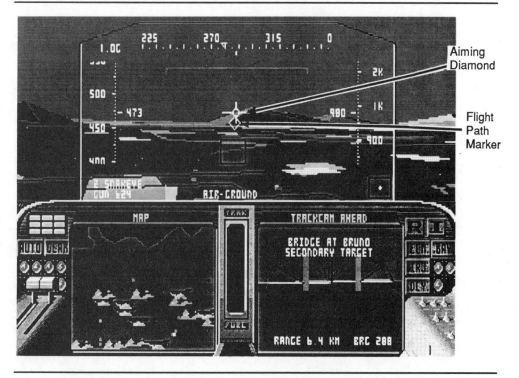

Figure 6-7. Flight Path Marker placed directly over the Aiming Diamond

5. When the Flight Path Marker is aligned with the HUD diamond and the Horizontal Ranging Bar becomes a single line, pickle two bombs by hitting the number two firing button on the joystick or by pressing the ENTER key. Close the bay doors by pressing **8**.

High-drag bombs can be dropped at a much lower altitude because the bomb slows down after release, allowing the attacking aircraft to escape the blast. This lower altitude makes the high-drag pass a much better option in a high-threat environment because you do not need to climb above 3,000 feet to release the weapon.

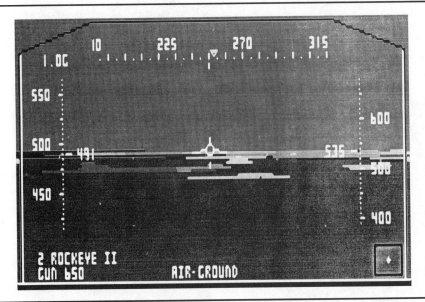

Figure 6-8.   HUD laser-guided bomb symbology prior to FLIR/Optics sensor lock-on

Laser-Guided Bombs

Laser-guided bombs used by the F-19 are the GBU-12, the CBU-72, and the Mk-20 Rockeye II. These bombs require you to fly a very precise attack profile (described next) or you will lose your laser lock on the target and the bombs will go stupid.

1. Call up the air-to-ground mode of the HUD with the F2 key. Press the SPACEBAR until the weapon of choice appears in the bottom-left corner of the HUD. Figure 6-8 shows the HUD symbology for an Mk-20.

2. Lock the FLIR/Optics sensor on to the target by hitting the / key until the right MFD display shows the target. When using laser-guided bombs, the right MFD shows the target, bearing, and range to the target and will also give you the same "missile lock" indication that you get with an AGM. In addition the display will also show if the sensor is locked on to a primary or secondary target. The left MFD in Figure 6-9 shows the FLIR/Optics sensor locked on to the secondary target.

3. Approach the target at 500 feet. At 8 kilometers open the bay doors by hitting the **8** key and start a shallow climb of between 10-20 degrees.

4. Watch the right MFD for a missile lock indication. When you see it appear, pickle off a single bomb and start a gentle level turn away from the target. Figure 6-10 shows the F-19 HUD view just after pickle. The bay doors must stay open in order to keep your Laser Designator locked on to the target.

5. When you see the bomb impact, close the bay doors by pressing the **8** key.

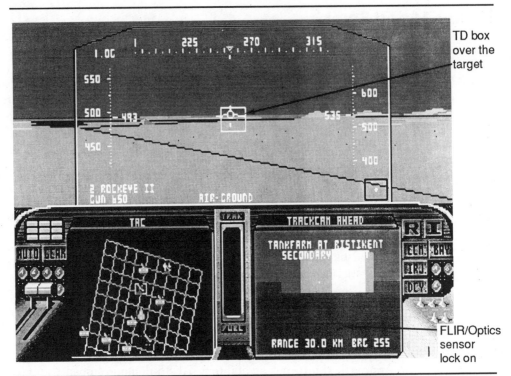

Figure 6-9. HUD laser-guided bomb symbology after FLIR/Optics sensor lock-on

Laser-guided bombs are very accurate and do not require precise target overflight like high-drag and low-drag bombs. The only difficult and critical part of the attack is the *designator turn* after bomb release. In this turn you must keep the belly of your jet facing the target for the bomb time of fall. Laser bombs guide on reflected laser energy; in the F-19 the source of this energy is the F-19 itself. In the bomb bay there is a Laser Designator that locks on to the target. This is why you must keep the bomb bay (located in the aircraft belly) pointed at the target through the bomb time of fall. This time is normally four to eight seconds depending on the range from the target when the bomb was released. Another important planning consideration when dropping laser-guided bombs is to note that you get 2

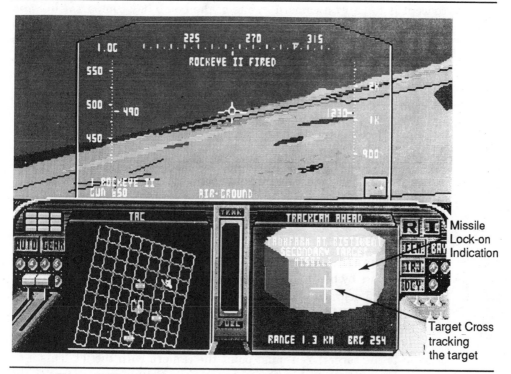

Figure 6-10. HUD view just after laser-guided bomb release

kilometer of range for every thousand feet of altitude of your jet. If you climb to 1,500 feet in your approach to the target, you will get a lock-on indication 3 kilometers from the target.

THE RECONNAISSANCE MISSION

Aerial reconnaissance is a related air-to-ground mission that is often combined with a bombing mission in the F-19 simulation. This mission is straightforward in concept but difficult to execute in the simulation. The concept is to carry a camera in one of the bomb bay compartments and overfly the target snapping a few pictures. The execution requires skillful flying and a very precise knowledge of F-19 aerial recon techniques. The following procedures will help you master this difficult mission:

1. Call up the air-to-ground mode of the HUD with the F2 key. Press the SPACEBAR until the 135-mm camera appears in the bottom-left corner of the HUD.

2. Lock the FLIR/Optics sensor on to the target by hitting the / key until the right MFD display shows the target. The display will show if the sensor is locked on to a primary or secondary target so you can tell if you are locked on to the correct reconnaissance target.

3. Approach the target at 500 feet. At 8 kilometers open the bay doors by hitting the **8** key, and start a shallow climb of between 5-15 degrees. When the bay doors open a Gun Cross will appear in the HUD.

The F-19 camera cannot be slewed (moved) and will not automatically lock on to the target! You must point the camera with the jet. This is in sharp contrast to the FLIR/Optics sensor (the F-19 manual refers to the FLIR/Optics sensor as a tracking camera). The FLIR/Optics sensor automatically locks on to targets and presents the pilot with a picture of the target in the right MFD. It also provides a Target Designator Box in the HUD and on the Tactical Display (which can be called up on the left MFD by pressing the F3 key). It cannot record these images, however, and cannot be used to photograph targets. When you open the bomb bay with the recon camera selected, the right MFD becomes the pilot's eye through the camera and the FLIR/Optics picture goes away. The bomb bay loaded camera has no brain and just points straight out the bomb bay. You see what the camera is looking at in the right MFD. The cross that appears down from the Gun Cross in the HUD gives the pilot an indication of where the F-19 aerial reconnaissance camera is pointing. Figure 6-11 shows the aerial reconnaissance camera HUD display.

4. Get lined up in azimuth (left-right) early in your approach to the target. The Camera Cross is down from the Gun Cross (which is on the F-19 roll axis) and if you roll the jet you will get a phenomenon that fighter pilots call the *pendulum effect*. This effect is caused when you roll the jet to line up and aim with a weapons reference below the roll axis of the aircraft. When you do this, your aiming reference will swing wildly in the HUD. Figure 6-12 shows how the pendulum effect works. The best way to avoid the pendulum effect is to fly the Flight Path Marker wings-level through the target. The Camera Cross will then follow smoothly and allow you to make a good pass. If you are in a bank when the Flight Path marker passes the target, you are in for Mister Toad's Wild Ride when you try to get the Camera Cross on the target.

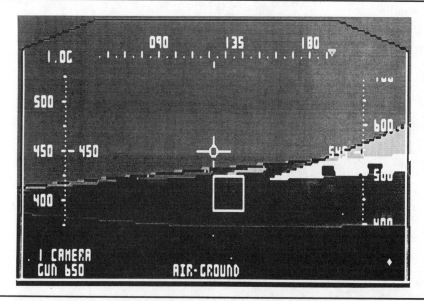

Figure 6-11. HUD view of camera symbology prior to bomb bay doors opening

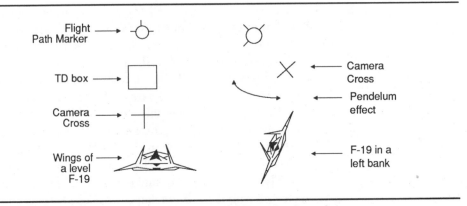

Figure 6-12.   Pendulum effect caused by F-19 bank angle

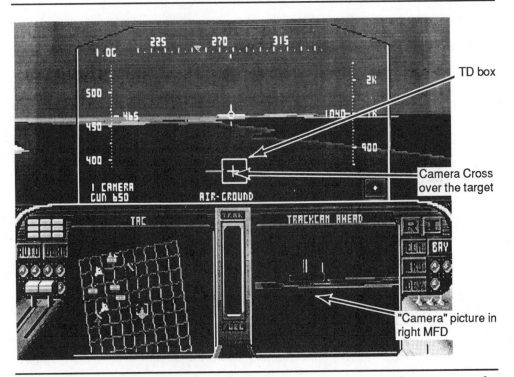

Figure 6-13.   HUD view of camera symbology after bomb bay doors are opened

5. When the Camera Cross reaches the target, hold it on the target by gently pushing forward on the stick. Look at the right MFD to ensure that the target is displayed, and snap some pictures by hitting the number 2 button on the joystick or the RETURN key if you are using the keyboard to fly. Figure 6-13 shows an F-19 HUD view of the camera lined up on the target. Notice the picture of the target in the right MFD. After you get at least one good picture, close the bomb bay doors by pressing the **8** key.

Aerial reconnaissance is one of the most challenging missions in the F-19 simulation. You must have in-depth systems knowledge and a high degree of flying skill to perform this mission with style and grace.

AERIAL RESUPPLY AND PICK UP

There are two additional missions that the F-19 can perform. These missions are aerial resupply and pick up. Aerial resupply can be executed by air dropping cargo or landing at a secret base and off loading cargo. The pick up mission requires the F-19 to land at a secret base and load cargo.

To land at a secret base, you must navigate using the normal way-point steering in the HUD and the Tac Display. There is no ILS transmitted from these secret bases. This is not difficult because the techniques discussed for landing in Chapter 3 do to rely heavily on ILS information. The only landing caution I will add for this mission is—do not get fast. The runways on these secret airstrips are only half as long as the normal runways. After landing, get right on the brakes to ensure you don't end up in a very flimsy, three-wheeled off-road vehicle. The last thing to remember before you take off again is to make sure your flaps are down. Taxi to the other end of the runway, turn around, and take off in the opposite direction that you landed in. This will give you the entire runway for takeoff.

Cargo is automatically loaded or unloaded when landing at one of these airstrips. A message in the HUD will tell you that this has occurred.

For aerial drop missions you can treat the cargo just like it was a bomb and pickle it off between 500—1,000 feet over the drop zone.

MUD BEATING

Beating up mud with bombs is hard work but somebody has to do it. Most fighter pilots would rather be shooting down MiGs and gaining fame and fortune than bombing ground targets in the teeth of the enemy defenses. Air-to-ground missions, however, are critical because they save the lives of our comrades and inflict grievous harm on our enemies. In the F-19 simulation the strike missions are the most challenging and fun parts so you must learn air-to-ground fundamentals to master the game. In the next chapter we will go beyond the fundamentals and discuss F-19 tactics.

7

SURVIVAL ON THE ELECTRONIC BATTLEFIELD

*"No one can tell another what to do in a future air-to-air fight.
We can only relate what we have done that
worked effectively in the past. In this game there
is a great demand for the individual who can 'play by ear'."*
From the Korean War tactics manual
No Guts — No Glory
written by Major "Boots" Blesse

A wise old Jedi Master once said, "Never underestimate the power of the Force." The Force in the *Star Wars* movies was an unseen power that gave warriors the ability to know what was going on around them and react correctly to the tactical situation. The Force guided their actions in complex battle situations, giving them an edge over their opponents. As a young(er) fighter pilot, I watched these movies and recognized instantly that "the Force" existed in fighter aviation as well. In fighter combat the Force is an elusive attribute that is stronger in some people than it is in others. We call this attribute *Situation Awareness* or *SA*. Fighter pilots with strong SA always know what is going on around them and react correctly based on this knowledge. To master the F-19, or any fighter aircraft, the pilot must have SA. Strong situation awareness is partly an accident of birth (like straight teeth and wavy hair); however, all fighter pilots can refine and hone their situation awareness. The rest of this book will help you strengthen the natural "Force" or SA that you possess.

To develop your situation awareness you must first know your enemy's capabilities and the capabilities of your jet and your ability to fly it. The jet, for example, is capable of flying down at 100 feet in the teeth of enemy defenses to dodge SAMs and shoot MiGs. However, if you are like me, you may not be able to fight at this altitude without hitting the ground. This type of self-knowledge is important when developing your SA. As we hone your SA, we will discuss the enemy and the tactical scenarios created in the F-19 simulation.

THE ENEMY

In the F-19 simulation, the enemy uses a form of Soviet Integrated Air Defense System (IADS), which consists primarily of Surface-To-Air missiles (SAMs) and fighters. All kills against your jet by the enemy are with SAMs fired from the ground or with air-to-air missiles fired from fighters. The SAMs are located at fixed sites in the enemy territory while the enemy fighters set up BARCAPs (BARrier Combat Air Patrols) at various positions along the route into the target. The enemy IADS in the F-19 simulation (and in the real world) has three primary attributes:

- Overlapping weapons systems
- Defense in depth
- Connectivity

Overlapping weapon systems and *defense in depth* together mean that the enemy uses a number of weapons systems with complimentary capabilities located at sites that give them the ability to engage penetrating aircraft with multiple systems simultaneously.

Connectivity means that if you are detected and engaged by one system, others will be alerted and will know where you are, based on the information passed to them by the first system that detected you.

To engage and shoot down the F-19, the enemy must first detect you. Once detection occurs, they will engage you with a missile fired from a SAM site or a fighter. Detection in the F-19 simulation occurs the same way that it does on the modern battlefield—with radar systems. Ground- and air-based radar systems probe the sky looking for targets. Once the target is detected, a different radar at the same location is used to track and engage the target. The F-19 aircraft is, of course, designed to deny (or at least delay) enemy detection. In this chapter we will discuss the enemy's capabilities to detect and engage your jet and the specific countermeasures and tactics you can employ to negate the enemy defenses.

Surface-to-Air Missiles (SAMs)

There are several types of SAMs represented in the simulation. It is not important to remember all the different types of SAMs and their individual characteristics. All you need to know is how SAMs engage your jet. The two basic types of SAMs facing your F-19 are radar- and Infrared- (IR) guided SAMs. All of the radar-guided SAMs use an acquisition radar to find your jet, and then a tracking radar to provide precise guidance information to the missile. The IR SAMs can also use an acquisition and tracking radar to fire at your jet, but once the IR SAM is off the rail (fired), it self-guides to the target, honing on the IR energy generated by the target's engine.

It is not important for the pilot to know specific guidance techniques, such as beam riding and semi-active guidance, employed by the various SAMs in the simulation. The F-19 pilot must understand, however, the difference between pulse and Doppler radars in the simulation since many tactics and countermeasures from our bag of tricks will work against one type of missile guidance but not against the other.

Pulse Radars

What you do need to know is that in the F-19 world there are *pulse* and *Doppler radars*. Pulse radars send out a radar signal that bounces off the target and then returns to the radar, giving the operator a signal or "blip" that can be tracked. It is a very straightforward system that has a big drawback: Mother earth is the biggest target out there and if the radar hits the earth it gets a very large return called *ground clutter,* which blinds the radar. A target aircraft can cause this type of radar problem for the pulse radar by just flying close to the ground. The ground clutter that the pulse radar has to deal with is affected by two variables: how close the target is to the ground and how far the target is from the site.

You can think of a radar beam as being similar to the beam of light from a flashlight. As the beam gets farther away from the transmitting source (in this case your flashlight) it gets wider and spreads out. A radar beam does the same thing. Any time that the beam comes in contact with the ground, it reflects ground clutter back to the radar site. The closer to the ground you fly, the harder it is to keep the beam from hitting the ground. Also, at long range the beam gets wider, and there is a higher probability of it hitting the ground and reflecting back clutter.

Pulsed radars, therefore, have a much better chance of tracking a target close to the site because at close range their beams are tighter and less likely to hit the ground. Figure 7-1 shows how pulse radars operate and what happens if their beams hit the ground. Notice that at close range the radar beam has less ground clutter problems against a low-flying aircraft.

Doppler Radars

Doppler radars operate in many ways like pulse radars. They send out a beam that hits the target and then returns to the radar. Unlike simple pulse radars, however, these radars not only look for a return signal, they also look at the frequency of the return signal. A Doppler radar signal goes out and hits an approaching target, for example, which causes the radar waves that return to the site to be bunched up. This is a result of the target's closing velocity on the radar site. Figure 7-2 shows how this occurs.

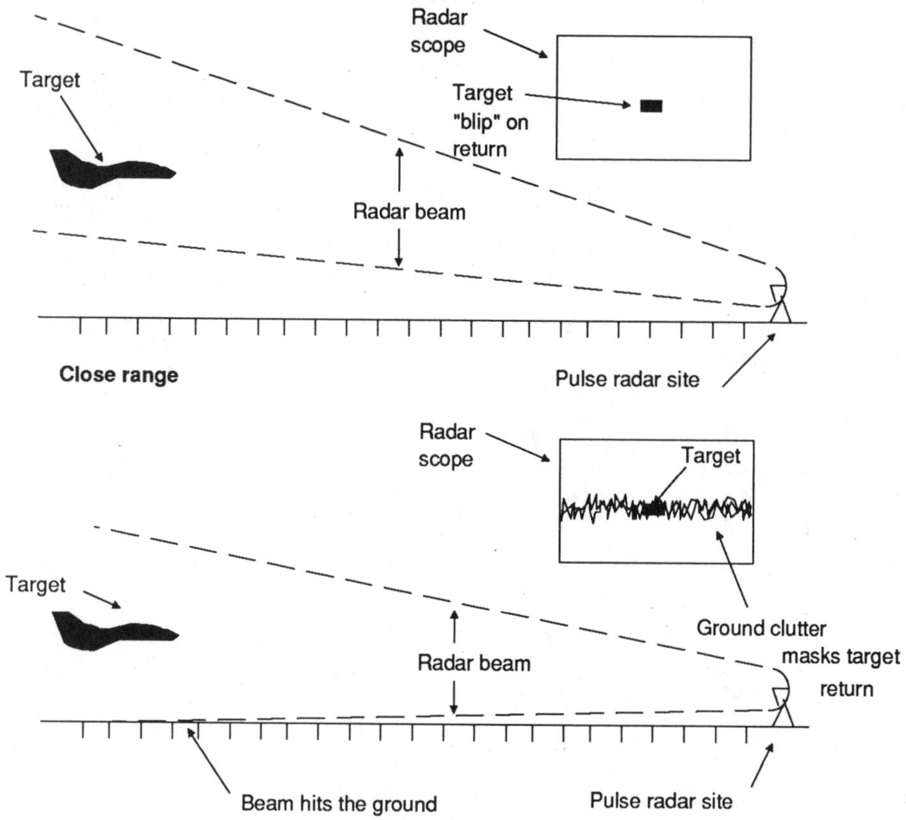

Radar
scope

Target
"blip" on
return

Target

Radar beam

Close range

Pulse radar site

Radar
scope

Target

Ground clutter
masks target
return

Target

Radar beam

Beam hits the ground

Pulse radar site

Figure 7-1. Pulse radar site

The Doppler radar uses this change in radar frequency to measure the target vector (speed and direction) and to track the target. If the target is flying away from the radar, an opposite Doppler shift occurs. The waves coming back to the radar are more spread out than the waves that the radar is sending out. Again this information is used by the radar to track

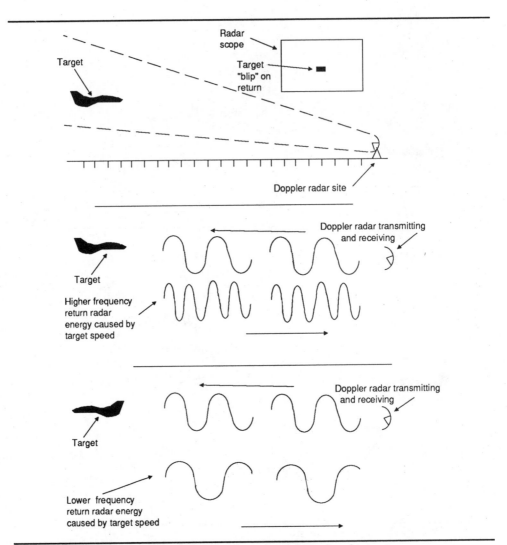

Figure 7-2. Doppler radar site detecting inbound and targets

the target. Figure 7-2 also shows this type of Doppler shift. A Doppler radar can "see" targets coming toward it or going away from it very easily, even amidst ground clutter, because when a Doppler radar hits the ground, the return signal shows no Doppler shift since the ground is not moving. The radar omits from the scope those signals that return without a Doppler shift, enabling the operator to see low-flying targets. This is both the strength and weakness of Doppler radars. If you turn to *beam* a Doppler radar (turn to place it either on your three or nine o'clock position as shown in Figure 7-3), the Doppler return from your jet will have the same return

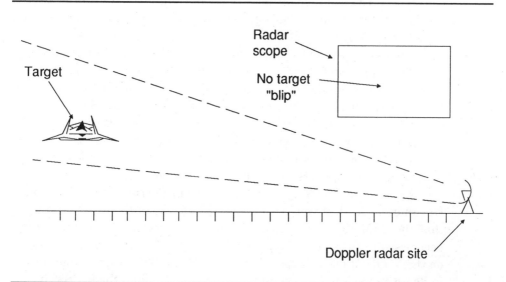

Figure 7-3.   Doppler radar unable to see beaming target

as the ground and the radar will not see or track your aircraft. That's the good news. The bad news is that if you are not beaming the radar site, these radars will track your jet down into the trees. It is very difficult to underfly a Doppler radar or to cause it to lose track unless you place the radar on the beam.

Is it Pulse or Doppler?

All radar SAMs and many of the IR SAMs use pulse and Doppler radars to detect and track targets. You can tell which type of radar is looking at you by looking at the Map Display on the left MFD. You get there by hitting the F3 key until the colored Map Display appears. This display and the Tactical Display are called up alternately on the left MFD by hitting the F3 key. (The Tactical Display has icons representing ground and air targets overlayed on grid lines.) You will see on the Map Display either dotted or solid lines coming from SAM sites that are emitting radar energy. The dotted lines denote a pulse radar while a solid line shows a Doppler radar.

This same symbology is used to show radar types on the maps shown during your pre-mission intel briefing. When you select Radar Sites on the Intelligence Briefing page you will get a map view of the SAM sites and either dotted or solid lines showing the detection range of the radar system.

The other way to tell which radar type is looking at you is to memorize which SAM types are located at specific sites and the characteristics of the SAM located at that site. For example, you would have to know that an SA-12 is a Doppler SAM system and is located at Tripoli. When this radar transmits or fires at you, a message will appear in the HUD telling you that the SAM site at Tripoli is shooting. Because I have spent the last decade strapped to various types of big and ugly flying machines with guns on them, I don't use this technique. I have found that there is no time for in-depth analysis in the cockpit, and I religiously follow the KISS principle in air combat (KISS stands for Keep It Simple, Stupid). Trying to remember all of the different SAM characteristics and sites is too complicated for most fighter pilots, and this technique will fail you when you need it most. The best technique for SAM identification is to just remember that solid lines are Doppler radars, and dotted lines are pulse radars. It's too bad our computers don't dispense a banana when we get it right. That would ensure that the fighter pilots I know would learn it fast.

Enemy Fighters

There is a long list of aircraft that you will come up against in the F-19 simulation. All enemy aircraft will try to find you with pulse or Doppler intercept radars and will then close the range and shoot you with either an IR- or radar-guided missile. The real difference between dealing with enemy fighters and enemy SAMs is that enemy fighters can mass their forces once they find you, while SAMs are stuck in fixed locations. Fighters in most ways are more dangerous and complicated to deal with because of their mobility. You can think of an enemy fighter in the F-19 simulation as a mobile SAM site that follows you around, hosing missiles.

The missiles that are fired by enemy fighters have essentially the same characteristics as the ones fired from the ground. (Remember that Chapter 5 has a description of what to do when an enemy aircraft fires a missile at your jet.) The primary thing to remember is that if you are detected by enemy fighters, you can expect more of them to be drawn to your location; once an enemy fighter makes a visual identification of your jet (sees you), you must kill that jet or the bandit will kill you. You should take it very personally when an enemy fighter pilot like the Soviet SU-27 pilot shown in Figure 7-4 closes on your jet with violent intent. When this occurs, you must focus your attention on killing before you are killed.

SAM sites are manned by a bunch of ground "pounders" staring at radar screens while fighters are manned by fighter pilots like yourself. Air-to-air combat is nothing short of a test of courage as the fighter pilot brethren duke it out for control of a small patch of sky. The pounders in the SAM sites are dangerous but they are still pounders and can be beaten more easily than a fighter pilot (even in a simulation).

THE F-19

The F-19 is well equipped to survive the enemy IADS. The F-19 is not a maneuverable jet so F-19 pilots must lean heavily on situation awareness and high-technology threat countermeasures. The primary countermeasure to enemy threat systems is the jet's low Electromagnetic Visibility, or

Figure 7-4. Soviet pilot flying an SU-27

EMV. This term refers to how easily the jet can be "seen" by both enemy radar and IR systems.

EMV can be read out on an EMV gauge in the center of the cockpit. This indicator features a vertical bar that originates at the bottom of the gauge and moves up and down, showing aircraft EMV. The higher the bar, the greater the EMV, and the easier it is for the bad guys to find you. Figure 7-5 shows this gauge in the cockpit. Enemy radar emissions are shown on this same gauge and appear as vertical bars or strobes coming from the top of the gauge. Enemy aircraft search radars come down the right side of the gauge and enemy ground-based search radars come down the left side of the scope. If an enemy strobe and the F-19 EMV bar intersect, a audio warning tone will sound, indicating that the aircraft EMV is big enough to be detected by the enemy radar. This does not necessarily mean that your jet has been detected. Usually it will take a few radar hits in order for the enemy to find you.

EMV can be controlled by the pilot in several ways. The following is a list of the things that affect F-19 EMV:

- *Altitude* The lower the altitude, the lower the EMV.

- *Bank angle* The greater the bank angle, the higher the EMV.

- *Throttle position* The higher the throttle setting, the higher the EMV.

- *External devices* Anything hung out into the wind (such as gear, flaps, speed brake, bomb bay doors) increases EMV.

- *Radar-jamming pod* If the pod is on, you have the EMV of an aluminum-coated barn door.

You can check the effect of these factors on EMV by watching the EMV gauge as you gain altitude or turn on your jamming pod, for example. The higher that vertical bar on the gauge gets, the greater your chance of witnessing a SAM or air-to-air missile fly-by.

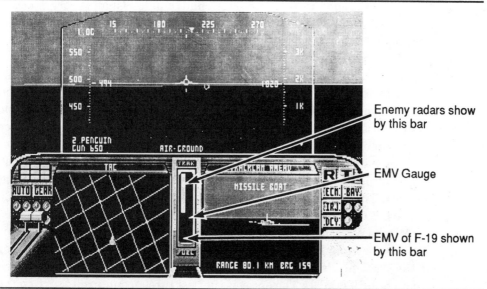

Enemy radars show by this bar

EMV Gauge

EMV of F-19 shown by this bar

Figure 7-5. EMV gauge

F-19 Countermeasures

The F-19 is jam-packed full of countermeasures to use against the enemy. The key to successfully employing these countermeasures is to first know their characteristics against the threat, and second, to have a technique to use against them that will work under pressure (remember the KISS principle). There are two main categories of countermeasures used in all fighters: expendables and on-board jammers. Expendables, as the name implies, are dropped from the aircraft. Jammers are carried on the jet and are used to foil enemy radar or IR systems by transmitting jamming energy.

The Expendables: Chaff, Flares, and Decoys

Chaff consists of tiny strips of metal that blossom into a small cloud upon release. This cloud masks your jet to an enemy radar system. You dispense chaff in the F-19 by hitting the **2** key. When dispensing chaff you will get an audio indication that you have released chaff, and you should also be able to see it on your Tactical Display (left MFD). F-19 chaff lasts two to three seconds, and the F-19 carries 18 chaff bundles. Chaff is very effective against all radar systems with an important caveat: you must place the missile or tracking radar on the beam against Doppler radar-equipped threats or chaff is as useless as diamond earrings on a pig.

Flares are pyrotechnic devices that give off heat and fool IR systems. You dispense flares in the F-19 by hitting the **1** key. Just as with chaff, you will get an audio indication when you drop a flare, and you will also be able to see it on the Tactical Display. The flares in the F-19 burn for two to three seconds and are effective against all IR threats. The F-19 carries 12 flares.

Decoys have both radar and IR signatures. When dropped by the F-19, they continue to fly along and slow down, drawing away enemy threat systems. The F-19 carries 3 decoys, which last anywhere from 15 to 60 seconds. While the decoy is alive, the letters DCY will be illuminated on the Missile Warning and Defenses panel to the right of the right MFD. This panel is shown in Figure 7-6. In addition, you can also observe the decoy on the Tactical Display in the left MFD. Figure 7-6 also shows a deployed decoy on the left MFD. The decoy is the best threat countermeasure on the

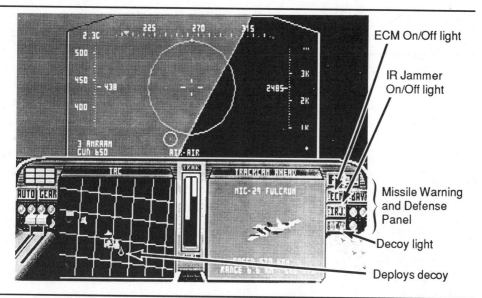

ECM On/Off light

IR Jammer
On/Off light

Missile Warning
and Defense
Panel

Decoy light

Deploys decoy

Figure 7-6. Missile Warning and Defenses Panel

jet but you have to know when to use them in order to get the most out of
your limited supply.

As a rule of thumb on all expendables, any time you drop one of them
you must turn at least 90 degrees, and if you are not already on a first
name basis with the gophers (down at low altitude), get there. Maintain
this new course for five to ten seconds and then turn back on normal course.
Always put some *G*s on the jet after dispensing chaff, flares, or decoys.

On-Board Jammers

The two types of on-board jammers used by the F-19 are the IR and radar
jammer. The radar jammer is also referred to as ECM or *Electronic
Countermeasures*.

The *IR jammer* is turned on by hitting the **3** key. Once activated, it
sends out pulses of intense IR energy that blind the seeker heads of IR
missiles. When the jammer is turned on, the IR indication on the Missile

Warning and Defenses panel, shown in Figure 7-6, illuminates. There is good news and bad news about all jammers (including the IR jammer on the F-19). The good news is that they do fool some missiles some of the time. The bad news is that the IR jammer in the F-19 cuts your available engine power by 15 percent. In addition, if left on for too long, it will shut off automatically, leaving you naked as a jaybird to incoming IR missiles (if you are depending on it exclusively). The last problem with this jammer is that it will act as a beacon to the newer IR missiles once they get in close.

The bottom line on this one is that you should only use this jammer in two circumstances in the F-19 simulation. The first one occurs when an IR missile has been fired and is at least one grid square (on the Tactical Display) away from your jet. In this case, turn on the jammer and, just as with the expendables, turn the jet 90 degrees and hold this new heading for five to ten seconds before resuming course. Once established back on the original course *turn the jammer off.* Figure 7-7 shows this maneuver. All enemy air-to-air and air-to-ground missiles have a 45 degree field-of-view. If you jam or decoy the missile and you maneuver out of this field-of-view, the missile will go stupid and miss you. The trick is to jam

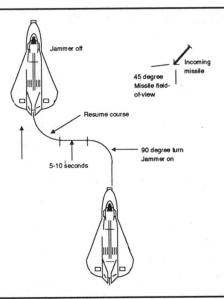

Figure 7-7. F-19 jamming maneuver

the missile, maneuver, and then turn off the jammer when you are outside the missile field-of-view. The use of the IR jammer increases your EMV significantly and if left on for too long it will draw an angry crowd in a really big hurry.

The second situation in which you could use the IR jammer is when an enemy aircraft fires a missile at you. In this case you need to turn to put the missile on the beam, drop chaff and flares, and turn on all of your jammers to include the IR jammer.

ECM, also called the radar jammer, is turned on by hitting the **4** key. When activated, the ECM pod puts out jamming that goes primarily against the *tracking* radar. When the jammer is on, the ECM light on the Missile Warning and Defenses panel illuminates. (This panel is shown in Figure 7-6.) ECM is more effective the farther you are away from the radar site. As you get in close, the power of the radar site is far greater than the power of your jamming so the site "burns through" the jammer. For this reason, just as with the IR jammer, you should use this jammer with discretion. In fact, just to keep it simple, I use the radar jammer the same way I use the IR jammer. When a radar missile is fired at your jet and is at least one grid square away on the Tactical Display, switch on your ECM and turn the jet at least 90 degrees for five to ten seconds. After getting back on heading, turn the ECM off. It's the same missile field-of-view reasoning as the IR jammer. Again, Figure 7-7 shows this maneuver.

F-19 Threat Warning

The F-19 has excellent threat warning systems. The first of these is the EMV gauge that we have already described. Above this gauge is the TRAK warning light shown in Figure 7-8. The EMV gauge shows the enemy's air- and ground-based search radars while the TRAK light illuminates to show that you are being tracked by an enemy radar system. When you see this light illuminated, you must immediately switch the left MFD to the Tactical Display. You do this by hitting the F3 key.

The reason you get into the Tactical Display is to see the incoming missiles that almost always follow the TRAK light. The best way to detect a missile launch on your F-19 is to see it on the Tactical Display, as shown in Figure 7-8. The other way is to turn toward the missile and try to pick

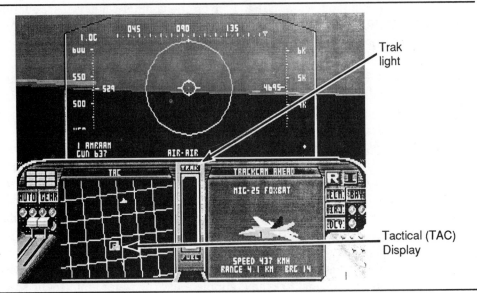

Figure 7-8. F-19 Tactical Display

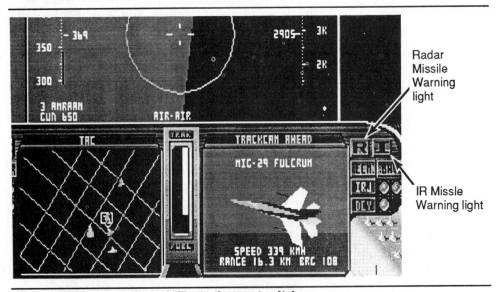

Figure 7-9. "R" and "I" missile warning lights

up a small red dot in your HUD. This red dot is the incoming missile and you will have an exciting and short life in the F-19 simulation if you use this technique for missile detection and avoidance.

Another very useful threat warning indication in the cockpit is the "R" and "I" warning lights shown in Figure 7-9. These lights illuminate to tell you which type of missile is in the air guiding on your jet. The "R" light indicates a radar missile and the "I" light indicates IR missiles. The light will stay illuminated as long as the missile is guiding on the F-19. If your countermeasures cause the missile to lose its lock-on, the light will go out. If more than one of these missiles is guiding on you, the light will stay on for as long as one of these missiles is following.

Here is a list of the F-19's primary threat warning systems:

- *The EMV gauge* is used for seeing search radars trying to detect your jet.

- *The TRAK light* shows when a radar is tracking the F-19.

- *The Tactical Display* gives the pilot a complete top down view of the battle including all of the missiles guiding on the F-19.

- *The "R" and "I" warning lights* illuminate to show that a radar or IR missile is guiding on your jet.

These systems are excellent and greatly enhance your situation awareness. There is more to SA, however, than just knowledge. Knowing what is going on around you must be followed up by *reacting* correctly. The next section will close the loop and discuss reacting to the tactical situation.

BATTLEFIELD SURVIVAL

To consistently survive in the F-19 simulation you must have a tactical game plan for dealing with the Integrated Air Defense System. It is hard to come up with a world-beating idea to defeat the enemy when the sky is full of missiles and you are down to your last 10 feet of altitude and 100 knots of airspeed. IADS, as we have already discussed, consists of a network of air- and land-based radar acquisition systems that are designed to detect incoming aircraft. Once they *detect* your jet they pass you off to another radar that *tracks* you. The threat system that is tracking you then *engages* you with a missile. I call this *the life cycle of an enemy engagement*. The F-19 pilot must have a tactical game plan that includes simple rules of thumb for handling each part in the enemy engagement life cycle.

The Detection Phase

One of the goals in every fighter mission is to *deny* the enemy a chance to detect your jet. Stealth aircraft such as the F-19 are well equipped to accomplish this goal. We have already talked about the pilot-controllable actions that reduce your EMV. The two primary ones are altitude and external devices; as you approach enemy territory you should be at 500 feet. At this altitude you are hard to detect but you are not so low that you have to focus all of your attention on flying the aircraft. As you head inbound, watch your EMV gauge for enemy radar strobes.

F-19 Rope-a-Dope

If a strobe is getting close to your EMV bar, you have three options:

- Flying lower
- Employ countermeasures
- Rope-a-dope

Flying lower is the simplest option, and should be tried first. Bump your altitude down to 300 feet and level off. Watch the enemy radar strobe and see how close it is coming to your jet (use the EMV gauge).

If it is still getting close, you will have to alter your route or employ countermeasures and drop chaff or a decoy. Before you start to maneuver, you should note the type of radar that is looking for you. If it is pulse radar, and flying lower is not working, then you must turn to put the radar on

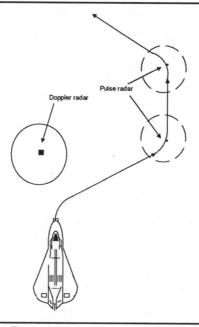

Figure 7-10.   F-19 Rope-a-dope

the nose to give it your smallest EMV profile (if the pulse radar is behind your three/nine line, then turn to put it directly at six o'clock). If it is Doppler radar you should turn to beam the site. I call this maneuver the F-19 *rope-a-dope,* and it is shown in Figure 7-10. (Keep in mind that this maneuver is used to deny the enemy acquisition of your jet. You must still continue to work your way to the target.)

The rope-a-dope is easy to execute when you are fighting a small number of SAM sites. The real trick is knowing what to do when you get yourself in the old General Custer situation. When radars are popping up all over and your brain is starting to short-circuit, remember these simple rules of thumb:

- Doppler radars are more deadly than pulse radars so react to a Doppler radar first.

- Doppler-equipped aircraft are generally more deadly than Doppler-equipped SAMs so react to the Doppler aircraft first.

- A Doppler-equipped threat of any kind has priority over a non-Doppler enemy SAM or fighter.

- If you are in a rope-a-dope threat reaction to a SAM that stops transmitting, discontinue the maneuver and continue the mission. Keep your head out and be ready to continue with your maneuver if it comes back to life.

The Chaff Burger

If you point at a pulse radar or beam a Doppler radar and it still detects you, it is time to feed the enemy radar a chaff burger. To confuse a pulse radar, climb quickly to 1,000 feet, drop a bundle of chaff by hitting the **2** key, and then return to 300-500 feet, pointing straight at the site (or directly away from it if it is behind you). For a Doppler radar, you can do the same maneuver except that you need to beam the site as you return to low altitude. Using this maneuver may cause the site to track your chaff while you slip past underneath.

Terrain Masking

A fighter pilot's best friend against radars is vertically developed terrain (hills and mountains). Any time you can get a piece of hard dirt between your behind and a search radar that is looking for you, do it, and do it quickly. Hiding in the terrain is called *terrain masking*. Radars cannot see through hills so as you ingress (fly into the target area) you should notice the terrain along your route of flight. If you're aware of the terrain, if the need arises, you can get behind a piece of it quickly. Remember that you must put the hill between your jet and the enemy radar to be effective. This breaks the radar's line-of-sight and will deny the enemy acquisition.

There is one important caveat to this technique. It takes a lot of computrons to simulate the effects of terrain on the threats. For this reason, in F-19, terrain masking is not always effective and you may be seen and engaged right through the hills and mountains. It is still a very good idea to use terrain masking since this technique is a standard fighter pilot procedure for fighting the enemy. Just don't be surprised if the enemy can see through the terrain.

The Tracking Phase

In most of the advanced levels of the F-19 simulation you can only delay enemy acquisition. The enemy will find you eventually, and when they do they will start tracking your jet. When you are being tracked, the "TRAK" above the EMV gauge will be illuminated. When this occurs, it is time to start some serious juking and jiving because it will not be long before a missile cruises by with your name on it. The tracking phase will normally start with your jet getting "hit" with several radar strobes. These strobes will give you an audio tone and a visual indication on the EMV gauge. These radar hits will be followed by the TRAK light. When you get the TRAK light you should execute the following steps:

1. Descend to 300 feet.

2. Put a Doppler threat on the beam and a pulse threat on the nose.

   - If you are not sure what kind of threat is tracking you then turn to place it on the beam (remember Doppler radars are more dangerous).

   - If you are not sure where the radar is that is tracking you, turn the jet 90 degrees from its present heading.

3. Turn on your ECM by pressing the **4** key. ECM should only be left on for short periods of time. After the track light illuminates you should turn your ECM on for about five seconds and then turn it off. If it does not break the tracking radar's lock-on within five seconds it probably is not going to, so leaving it on will only highlight your jet.

4. Call up the Tactical Display in the left MFD by pressing F3.

Note: If you keep hitting the ground when trying to fly at 300 feet then jack your altitude up to 500 or more feet. Flying into the ground is far more unhealthy than being tracked or even shot by an enemy missile.

The Engagement Phase

Despite your best efforts the enemy will eventually hose a missile at you. When a missile is in the air, you are in the engagement phase and must terminate your other activities and fight the missile. The following list of actions provides the Stealth pilot a complete missile defense procedure:

1. *Detect the incoming missile.*

2. *Put the closest missile guiding on your jet on the beam.*

3. *Go lower* (but no lower than 300 feet).

4. *Employ your countermeasures.*

5. *Pull max Gs and drop chaff and flares at missile end game* (defined shortly).

6. *Look for the next missile.*

Figure 7-11 shows a bird's eye view of the missile defense maneuver.

Detect the incoming missile   This first step is the most important in fighting a missile. You must detect the missile launch. This is very easy to do with the advanced avionics of the F-19. When you get a TRAK light above your EMV gauge, call up the Tac Display on the left MFD. You do this by pressing the F3 key until the Tac Display appears.

Remember: TRAK light — Tac Display. With the Tactical Display up you can now watch for missiles. When you see the missile on the Tactical Display, go on to the next step in the procedure.

Put the closest missile guiding on your jet on the beam   There is one universal truth about fighting missiles. This truth is — fight missiles with

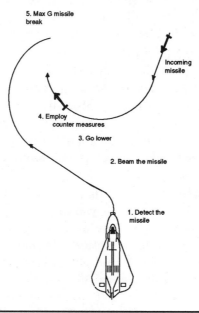

5. Max G missile
break

Incoming
missile

4. Employ
counter measures

3. Go lower

2. Beam the missile

1. Detect the
missile

Figure 7-11.   Bird's-eye-view of missile defense

aspect. What this means is that you must give an incoming missile an aspect problem, and all missiles have the biggest problem with beam aspect. To effectively fight a missile, you must place it on the beam (your three or nine o'clock position). This is the most important step in the engagement phase once you have confirmed the missile launch.

In the F-19 simulation, placing an incoming missile on the beam does three important things for you. First, it gives all missiles, including the most deadly missiles in the simulation, Doppler missiles, the worst tracking problem. Second, once you turn to put an incoming missile on the beam you can easily see on the Tactical Display if it is guiding on your jet or not. If the missile is on your nose or tail you cannot tell if your maneuvers and countermeasures are working. If the missile is on the beam and your defense is working, the missile will start to drift aft and away from your jet. The last reason you place all incoming missiles on the beam is in case the missile arrives at *end game* (near your jet), your last ditch maneuver will be effective. We will cover the last ditch maneuver in more detail later.

Go lower   Getting to low altitude may trash the missile guidance. Even if it doesn't, it will lower your EMV and make you less vulnerable to the next missile. I use 300 feet as a "no lower than" altitude because I find it very difficult to fly below this altitude and still fight effectively in the F-19 simulation. Every pilot has their own minimum fighting altitude; yours may be higher or lower than mine. During this step in the missile defense game plan, go to your own personal minimum altitude.

Employ your countermeasures   As you get lower and are turning to put the missile on the beam, you should drop a chaff bundle and a flare. If you are sure what type of missile is being fired, you can just drop chaff for radar missiles and flares for IR-guided missiles. The "I" and "R" lights can be used to tell you which kind of missile is on the way, but be careful. These lights are most useful when you need them the least. If the sky is full of missiles, they are useless. If your missile defense technique is to look at these lights and drop either chaff or flares depending on whether or not the lights are on, then you are bound for the meat locker. It is far safer to drop one bundle of chaff and a flare as you maneuver to the beam.

ECM and the IR jammer can be used once you are established on the beam and the missile is still guiding. Use these jammers only if the missile is farther than one tactical grid square from your jet. If the missile is closer, don't fool with the jammers.

The last countermeasure you have is your three decoys. I use a decoy when I see that more than one missile is going to arrive at my jet at one time. You do not have many decoys so use them wisely. Remember, though, there is no need to die with extra chaff, flares, and decoys in the jet.

Pull max Gs and drop chaff and flares at missile end game   If the missile gets close to your jet you will hear a missile warning tone. When this happens you should roll the jet 45 degrees, while pulling maximum Gs. With your other hand you should dispense chaff and flares (by hitting the **2** and **1** keys). The missile will either pass by harmlessly or detonate. If the missile flies by or detonates and does not destroy you, go on to the next step.

Look for the next missile   If you are alive after the missile engagement, you need to watch for the next missile and get ready to go through your missile defense procedure again.

Battle Damage

If you are hit by an enemy missile you may or may not be seriously damaged. Serious damage will prevent you from performing your mission. After you have been hit you should continue to perform your missile defense until there are no more missiles guiding on your jet. At this point you can check your jet for damage. Call up the System Damage screen in the right MFD by pressing the F6 key. In addition, on the right side of the cockpit there is a panel of lights that warn the pilot of system damage. The System Damage screen in the right MFD and the warning lights on the left side of the cockpit are shown in Figure 7-12. With these warning systems, the pilot can quickly judge the degree of aircraft damage and what should be done about it.

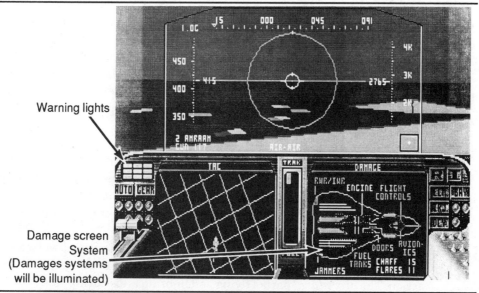

Figure 7-12.   Systems damage indicators in the F-19 cockpit

Aircraft damage that jams the bay doors open should be considered serious, and you should think twice about continuing the mission. Damage to your defense systems may also force you to abort the mission. Engine problems and flight stability problems can be overcome in most cases but you should perform a *controlability check* before deciding to continue the mission. During this check climb to 1,000 feet and make a few turns to check aircraft response. Move the throttle back and forth and check your engine response and thrust. Last, *check your fuel.* One of the worst battle damage injuries you can sustain is a massive fuel leak. If your fuel cells have been turned to Swiss cheese, you better "get out of Dodge" before you end up flying a cinder block (an F-19 with a flamed-out motor actually flies worse than a cinder block).

The bottom line on battle damage is that you have to access what you've lost and then make a call based on the tactical situation. Remember to keep fighting the incoming missiles first and check for battle damage when you are disengaged from the threat.

FLYING AND FIGHTING

You may get the impression from all the "how to" lists presented in this chapter that air combat is very procedurally oriented. If you got that idea then you are correct. From takeoff to landing, a fighter pilot goes through a routine that ensures the correct action be performed at the correct time. These procedures also extend into the combat arena. A fighter pilot must have a tactical game plan when engaging the enemy. In this way a fighter pilot is like a wrestler. The pilot has a few moves down pat and when certain situations develop, he uses those moves. In this chapter I gave you some of my moves and the situations that I use them in. This will give you a foundation to build your own moves for other more complex combat situations.

At the beginning of this chapter we said that situation awareness is recognizing the correct course of action and then executing that correct action. The *procedural* part of flying and fighting is executing your "moves" against the enemy. The *perceptual* part of air combat is observing the tactical situation and then deciding which moves you should execute. Recognizing what to do is the tough part. There is no all-encompassing list of actions that cover every situation. As an F-19 pilot you have to analyze each unique situation, and then decide your course of action.

In the next chapter we will go through an F-19 mission and describe mission planning factors and pilot actions. This discussion will tie together our previous air-to-air, air-to- ground, and threat reaction discussions and hopefully give you the "big picture" on F-19 tactical employment.

8

F-19 TACTICS

"Untutored courage is useless in the face of educated bullets."
—General George S. Patton

Air combat tactics consist of a course of actions that allow pilots to survive the enemy threat and accomplish their mission. The emphasis of mission planning and execution is survival. When you strap yourself into the jet you should think first and foremost of getting yourself back to the bar (and into the company of an appreciative audience). Survival is the key objective on all fighter missions.

There is another important objective, however, and that is to destroy the target: at some point you will have to go in harm's way and get the job done. If no enemy defenses existed, you could place all your emphasis on destroying the target. Optimum weapons release conditions could be met on every delivery, and you could fly at slow airspeed at medium altitude to increase your chances of hitting the target. On the other side of the tactical equation, if you emphasized nothing but survival, you would go to the bar and not fly the mission at all. If you did fly, you would stay at very low altitude and high airspeed, and fly as far away from the threat as you could without considering the mission.

The tactical solution lies somewhere in between these extremes. Picture a scale depicting the balanced relationship between force survival and target destruction. The fighter pilot usually has to give up something on one side of the scale in order to get results on the other side. The key to effective combat flying is knowing when to favor one side of the scale in expense of the other side.

In the previous chapter, we talked about F-19 weapons employment and threat countermeasures. We also discussed fundamental F-19 threat reaction techniques. In this chapter, we'll review the entire mission, and see how all of these pieces fit together to make a complete F-19 balanced tactical game plan.

MISSION PLANNING

Each F-19 mission presents the pilot with a unique tactical situation. From the initialization menus you can select the area of the world in which you wish to fly, the level of conflict, the degree of skill of your adversaries, and the difficulty of your landings. The mission planning process remains the same, however, for all of these pilot-selectable starting conditions. After setting up the initial conditions, the Intel Briefing screen will appear. This screen is shown in Figure 8-1.

The Target

Most of this screen is a map view of the mission area. Direct ingress (route into target area) and egress (route out of target area) are shown with a flashing P and S marking your primary and secondary targets. From this display you should note the significant terrain along the route and the distance you will have to fly to accomplish your mission. Focus your attention on your primary target. The secondary target is just that — secondary. All mission planning starts at the primary target and works

CLASSIFIED   Mission Briefing   CLASSIFIED

PRIMARY MISSION 22

A terrorist leadership council is being held in one of their training camps. A well timed retaliatory strike will disrupt current operations and deter future terrorist acts. This opportunity may not occur again.

Your primary objective is to destroy the Camp at Al Badya, ONC VC47, before 21:00 hours.

SECONDARY MISSION 14

Washington has decided to get tough and hurt the opposition financially by destroying an oil storage facility. This will temporarily reduce oil exports, and hopefully force them to the bargaining table.

Your secondary objective is to destroy the Tank Farm at Al Badya, ONC VC37.

Press Selector to continue

Figure 8-1. Intelligence Briefing screen

backwards, so after a look at the large Intel map display you should call up the target description screen.

To get your primary and secondary target briefing, move the cursor over to the words "Mission Targets." Figure 8-1 shows where this is located on the Intel Briefing screen. Use the joystick or the ↑ or ↓ arrow keys to select the Mission Targets line and hit the number one release button on the joystick or the ENTER key to select it. You are now in the Mission Targets page shown in Figure 8-2. This screen will explain the political situation and tell you the targets and mission type. The targets are usually normal air-to-ground enemy assets such as bridges (or aircraft for air-to-air missions), and the missions against these targets can be attack, recon, or air resupply.

After your target briefing, select Exit at the bottom left corner of the Mission Targets screen and press the ENTER key. You will return to the Intel Brief screen, and you can start to study the threat picture.

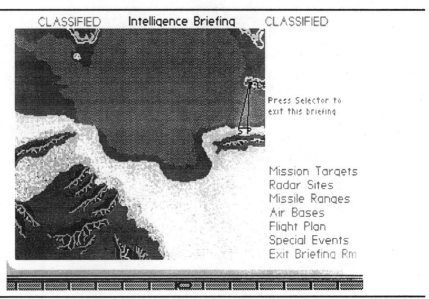

CLASSIFIED   Intelligence Briefing   CLASSIFIED

Press Selector to
exit this briefing

Mission Targets
Radar Sites
Missile Ranges
Air Bases
Flight Plan
Special Events
Exit Briefing Rm

Figure 8-2.   Mission Targets page

Electronic Order of Battle (EOB)

Now that you know the approximate position of your targets, you need to analyze what fighter pilots call the *electronic order of battle.* In the F-19 simulation this means that you study the position and type of all enemy radars arrayed against you. Use the Intel Briefing screen to do this by moving the cursor over the Radar Sites line and pressing the ENTER key. The radars will appear on the Intel map, with a circle showing their *detection range.* The ingress and egress route will still be shown on the map so that you can see which radars will be a factor in your mission.

Radars that will affect your flight should be further analyzed. To do this press the joystick left or right or use the ← or → arrow keys to step to the different radar sites. When you step to a radar site, the circle around the site will flash and an information block will appear in the upper-right corner of the Intel Brief screen describing the capabilities of the weapon system associated with the selected radar. Again, remember you can tell the Doppler radars by their solid lines and the pulse radars by their dotted lines (radar type is also written in the weapon description in the top-right corner of the screen).

Studying the EOB is a critical part of any fighter mission. During this phase the pilot forms an ingress and egress plan. To plan your route, use the following rules-of-thumb:

1. Avoid the threat by flying around the sites.

2. Plan a route that places the Doppler radars at your three and nine o'clock positions.

3. Go straight at the pulse radar threats when you cannot fly outside their detection range.

4. Use terrain masking whenever possible.

Note: You should plan your ingress and egress route while looking at the Intel Briefing page with the radar sites depicted.

The route that is shown on the map is usually not the route you should fly into the target. The computer generally gives you a route that takes you straight at the target — regardless of the threat. This "hey diddle diddle, right up the middle" approach will generally get you in big trouble. To avoid getting a face full of missiles as you cross into enemy territory, you should plan your own route into the target area based on the rules we have just outlined and your own tactical perspective.

The other Intel Briefing options are Missile Ranges, Air Bases, Flight Plan, and Special Events. None of these are particularly important except Special Events. If you select this option, small squares will appear on the Intel map showing areas of enemy concentrations that you should avoid (unless you enjoy dodging IR missiles).

The Missile Ranges selection is not important because radar detection range for SAMs in the F-19 simulation is always shorter than missile range. If a radar cannot find you, it cannot shoot you—so it doesn't matter how far its associated missile can shoot. If the radar can find you, you can bet your buns that the missile has the range to reach out and touch you. Air Bases gives the pilot the position of the enemy airfields and the type of aircraft located on them. Because the Air Order of Battle (AOB) is so dynamic, information on enemy airfields is not very helpful. Any number of aircraft can show up in any location on the battlefield regardless of where their airfields are located.

So before leaving the Intel Briefing page you should accomplish the following tasks:

1. Mark the position of the primary and secondary targets on the map, and note any significant terrain in the area.

2. Select Mission Targets and get a target description briefing.

3. Call up the Radar Sites option and note the detection range, location, and type of radars along your intended route.

4. Select Special Events and note the location of the small squares on the map display. These are areas of heavy enemy activity and should be avoided.

5. Plan an ingress and egress route that avoids threat as much as possible and that takes advantage of enemy radar gaps and limitations.

After getting a mind's-eye-view of your ingress route using the Intel Briefing screen, select the Exit Briefing Room option at the lower-right corner of the screen.

Weapons

After exiting the Intel Briefing screen, the Armament screen comes into view. The Armament screen is shown in Figure 8-3. The screen will appear with some computer-selected weapons already loaded into the F-19 bomb bays. These choices are rarely optimum for the tactical situation; you usually need to change them to match your capabilities and tactical game plan. The F-19 simulation has a wide array of targets and an equally large choice of weapons to engage these targets. For air-to-ground targets you have a choice of missiles, low-drag bombs, high-drag bombs, and laser-guided bombs, all of which come in a variety of flavors. In Chapter 4, we discussed each of these weapons and the targets they were good against.

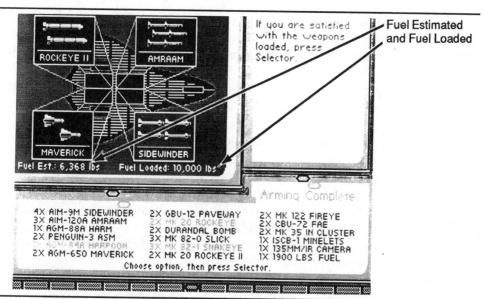

Figure 8-3. Armament screen

There is no perfect weapon choice for a given tactical situation, but again there are a few rules of thumb that will help you choose which weapons to load on the jet. Since our primary mission goal is surviving the mission, we choose our weapons with this in mind.

The first thing to do is pick weapons to destroy the primary and secondary target. If the target is a building, a radar, fuel tanks, or a mobile radar, I always pick Mavericks. The Maverick missile is the most flexible weapon in the simulation because it allows you to stand off from the target and can be used on almost any target on the battlefield. The *launch and leave* Maverick provides a minimum exposure attack profile because it can be fired at 500 feet, and immediately after launch you can maneuver the jet. For this reason, if the target can be destroyed by a Maverick, then I carry a Maverick.

If the target is a bridge, bunker, or other reinforced structure that a Maverick has a low Pk (probability of kill) against, then I use Mk-82 Snakes (a high-drag munition). This weapon requires you to overfly the target. It also demands concentration to line up and release the weapon (compared to the Maverick) but you do not have to climb out of the weeds to use it; it provides the second most survivable attack profile. For special targets, use special weapons. For example, sub pens require FAE, and you will need to use Durandels against runways. Since these two weapons are high-drag bomb types, they provide the same excellent low-attack profile as the Mk-82 Snake.

Once you pick weapons for your primary and secondary targets, the rest of the weapons that you load will be for self-preservation. Enemy aircraft comprise the biggest threat to your mission so always load AIM-120 AMRAAMs if they are available. The AMRAAM has excellent range and gives you a long lance to poke enemy aircraft before they can get close to you (and reach you with their lance). If you have room, you should carry Sidewinders along with AMRAAMS. This will give you the long lance *and* a close-in weapon for air-to-air combat. If you only have room for one type of missile, however, load AMRAAMs.

On recon missions you must carry a camera. Other special missions also require special cargo that takes up space in your bomb bays.

The bottom line on armament selection is that you think about survival first when selecting weapons to kill your primary and secondary targets. After selecting these weapons load up on air- to-air missiles. The only tough choice I have is between Sidewinders, Mavericks, or a HARM missile. After loading the weapons to attack my primary and secondary target (sometimes the same weapon can be used to destroy both targets), I normally make a judgment call on what will be the biggest threat along my route. If there is an SA-10 or SA-12 that I cannot beam during the ingress or egress then I will load a HARM rather than the Sidewinders. If there is a number of pulse Doppler-equipped missile boats along the way then I will load Mavericks instead of the Sidewinders. I usually choose Mavericks over Penguins or Harpoons in this situation because Mavericks are more flexible. If the missile boats do not become a factor then I can use the Maverick against ground-based radars. Most of the time, however, I go with Sidewinders since enemy fighters are the biggest threat.

All of these rules are purely my own personal technique. It is not important that you choose your weapons the same way that I do. The only important point is that you have a tactical game plan and choose weapons to match your plan.

Fuel

On the Armament screen shown in Figure 8-4 you will notice a Fuel Estimated and Fuel Loaded reading below the bomb bays. Before exiting the Armament page you should check these numbers and ensure that the *Fuel Loaded* exceeds the estimated *Fuel Required* amount to fly the mission. If you do not have enough gas, load the extra fuel tank available in the Armament screen. This tank will give you an extra 1,900 pounds of gas. If even this isn't enough, you can still fly the mission but you need to ingress at low airspeed (below 300 knots) to save fuel. The estimated fuel figure shown on this screen assumes that you will fly at high speed for the entire mission. Be sure you check your fuel available before climbing into the cockpit. To get into the cockpit, move the cursor over to Arming Complete and hit the ENTER key or the number one button on the joystick.

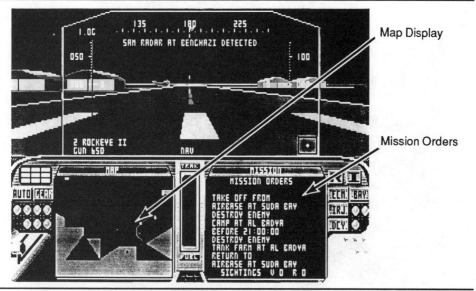

Map Display

Mission Orders

Figure 8-4. First F-19 MFD screens shown

Cockpit Set Up

Upon entering the cockpit you will see a display like the one shown in Figure 8-4. On the left MFD you will get a Map display, and on the right MFD you will get your mission orders. Prior to lowering your flaps and running up the power for takeoff, you should set the cockpit up for combat. The first thing to do is press the F7 key and bring up the Select Waypoint screen on the right MFD. This screen is shown in Figure 8-5. The Waypoint screen lists the points the computer has selected for us to fly to perform the mission. Waypoints 2 and 3 on the route are the primary and secondary targets, and waypoint 4 is homeplate (landing field).

Waypoint 1 is a point along the route into the target. You should move this point to match your ingress route (which you planned while studying the Intel Briefing screen). To move waypoint 1 around to match your ingress plan, press and hold down the F8 key, and then move the point with the ↑, ↓, ←, → arrow keys on the numeric keypad. You can observe the movement of the waypoint on the left MFD map display.

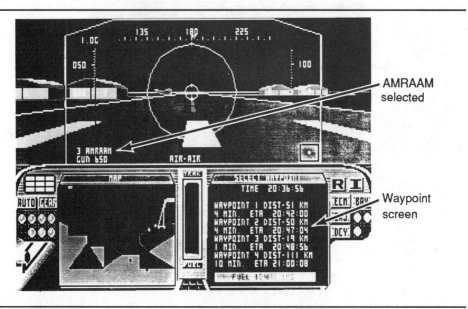

Figure 8-5.   F-19 ready for takeoff with Map Display and Waypoint Displays called up

Once you have placed waypoint 1 in a position that allows you to execute your ingress plan, select your weapons. Before taking off you should always be in a weapons delivery mode. Usually the first threats you will encounter will be enemy aircraft so select the air-to-air HUD mode by pressing the F2 key until "AIR-AIR" appears at the bottom of the HUD. Next call up your AMRAAMs (or Sidewinders if you are not carrying AMRAAMs) by hitting the SPACEBAR until the desired weapon appears in the lower-left corner of the HUD.

The last thing to do before takeoff is to watch the Map display and get another quick look at the EOB before blasting off. The Map display will show the radars that are transmitting, which will give you an idea of the status of the enemy radars along your route before takeoff. Figure 8-5 shows your cockpit ready for takeoff, with AMRAAMs selected.

MISSION EXECUTION

The planning stage is over, and it's time to fly the mission. From this point on you will have to execute your game plan as closely as possible and call audible when the tactical situation changes. After takeoff you should climb up to 500 feet, clean up the jet (raise the gear and flaps), and then engage the autopilot by hitting the **7** key. With the autopilot engaged, the aircraft will climb to 500 feet (if it is at a lower altitude) or it will stay at the altitude it was flying when the autopilot was engaged. In addition, the autopilot will steer the jet towards the next waypoint (which just after takeoff is waypoint 1). The autopilot will *not* follow terrain, so be careful when approaching mountains. You will have to grab the stick and "hand fly" the aircraft to keep from turning the jet into scrap metal. When you grab the stick, the autopilot will automatically disengage. To reengage it you need to press the **7** key again.

With the autopilot on, you can concentrate on watching the Map display and your EMV gauge. The whole idea on the ingress is to delay detection, so stay low and avoid contact with the enemy as long as possible. A good way to focus the big evil eye of the enemy on your jet is to shoot at nonthreatening enemy targets on the ingress. If the enemy is not threatening you, don't let your fangs jut out so far that you trip over them. In other words, don't engage the enemy on the ingress until the enemy engages you.

Enemy Fighters

As you enter enemy airspace you will likely encounter enemy fighters. The first indication you will have that bandits are in the area is their search radars appearing on the F-19 EMV gauge. Enemy fighters are a serious threat during ingress and very difficult to sneak past. The best course of action when you pick an enemy fighter radar strobe on your EMV gauge is to call up the Tactical display on the left MFD by pressing the F3 key. Once the display is called up, carefully monitor the position of the enemy fighter and have your longest range missile ready. Lock the FLIR/Optics sensor on the closest enemy bandit by placing the target on the nose and hitting the / key. After lock-on go back to course. If the enemy fighter does not detect you, continue on course. If enemy radar starts to hit your jet, and you are detected, then advance on the fighter. Turn the jet immediately to get the target on the nose, and when you get a missile lock indication in the right MFD, pull the target inside the Missile Reticle in the HUD and shoot. Keep your defensive guard up by watching the Tac display for a missile shot by the enemy. If the bandit hoses one off at you, then you need to go through your missile defense procedures (discussed in the previous chapter). If your missile doesn't toast the bogey then close in for a gun attack.

Multi-Bogey Engagements

The real challenge as you ingress to the target is dealing with a formation of two or more enemy fighters. Fighting more than one bandit at a time is called a *multi-bogey engagement*. When this occurs, you need to engage as many bandits as you can before they close into visual range. To do this, lock the FLIR/Optics sensor on the closest bandit and then turn to put him on the nose. Call up your longest range missile and shoot when you get a missile lock indication in the right MFD.

As soon as the missile is off the rail, hit the **B** key to lock the FLIR/Optics sensor on the next closest target in the formation. If the sensor locks on to the wrong bandit, just keep hitting the **B** key until you get the correct target. When you get a missile lock indication, shoot. If the second bandit that you are engaging has closed into Sidewinder range, then shoot a Sidewinder and do not waste a long-range AMRAAM (assuming you are carrying both types of missiles). Keep closing the range, and hope the Pk god (probability of kill god) is on your side. If the Pk god is with you, your missiles will shred the target and even the odds. If the Pk god turns against you, push the throttle up to full power and get ready for a "fur ball" (maneuvering fight).

The Escape Window

In all air-to-air fights the fighter pilot must be aware of his escape window. You can think of the escape window as your safe path out of an aerial engagement. When you are undetected by the enemy, your escape window is the size of an airplane hanger and you can easily fly through it and disengage at any time. When the bandit detects your jet and starts to close, your escape window shuts down. When a bandit in F-19 gets a *visual ID,* or VID, on your jet, the escape window becomes the size of a postage stamp. There is no way out of the fight when a bandit sees you because the F-19 cannot outrun most enemy fighters. When a bandit gets a VID someone is bound for the meat locker. Just make sure that someone is not you.

The best way to keep an escape window open is to avoid being detected by the bandit. Once you are detected by enemy radar your escape window starts to close, and it shuts down entirely when a bandit has a VID. When a bandit finds your jet with radar you can use a decoy and turn to counter the radar (beam a Doppler radar or put a pulse radar on the nose or tail). You may be able to slip through a small crack in the escape window by using this technique. If you are out of bullets and missiles or low on gas, you may have no choice. If you have weapons and fuel on the jet, however, it is best to engage and kill a bandit that has detected your F-19. Just remember, in air-to-air combat always be aware of where you are in relation to your escape window and don't get any valuable appendages caught in the window when it slams shut.

Enemy SAMs

Enemy SAMs are not as dangerous as enemy fighters because they will not follow or gang up on you. If you are engaged by a SAM it is best to defeat the missile and then continue on the mission. On select occasions, though, you may have to engage a SAM with a missile (HARM, Maverick, Penguin, or Harpoon). The following is a list of conditions that may lead you to engage the SAM site rather than avoid it:

- A Doppler SAM is located along your ingress route and you cannot beam it because you will run out of gas flying around it. You'll have to destroy this SAM or risk getting speared by it as you fly by it.

- Several Doppler-equipped SAMs with overlapping coverage are located along your route and while beaming one of them another one will probably detect and hose you. In this particular case, one of them has to go.

- A SAM is located *with* the target (within 10 kilometers). You are better off killing the SAM first so you won't end up doing your "funky chicken" missile defense in the middle of the attack.

- You are almost out of enemy territory, and you're feeling kind of mean and in the mood to kill something. Before giving in to blood lust, make sure you really are close to "getting out of Dodge." I have gotten my rear end shot off doing this, so be careful.

The only reason I even mention that last one is because I know what it is like to have your fangs scraping the keyboard. If you have to tear into something (rather than getting up from your computer and kicking your dog), go ahead and go for the points, and take on that SAM site as you egress enemy territory.

The Target

You should plan and execute a target attack that minimizes your exposure to the threat. To accomplish this, fly low and come into the target on a flight path that keeps you away from enemy defenses. Before takeoff you looked at the threat and planned the best route to the target. Once you're airborne, however, the threat picture might change as enemy fighters appear and radar sites are destroyed or shut down. When the tactical situation changes you need to change your route of flight to adapt. You do not have to fly directly at the target. Use your Map and Tactical display to get a threat picture and maneuver to avoid the enemy whenever possible.

When you get your target briefing before the mission you should note the "no later than" time that some missions have for target attack. When you call up the Select Waypoint screen on the left MFD (by pressing the F7 key), there will be an ETA (or estimated time of arrival) time shown to the right of each waypoint. Figure 8-6 shows an F-19 en route to the target with the Select Waypoint screen called up on the right MFD. You can see the times associated with each waypoint. These times tell you when you will arrive at each waypoint given your current airspeed, and are constantly updated. If you get delayed while ingressing into the target area you should check this time to make sure you can get to your target within your attack window. If you are late, accelerate to make up time (if fuel allows). If you don't have the gas then just do the best you can. In the F-19

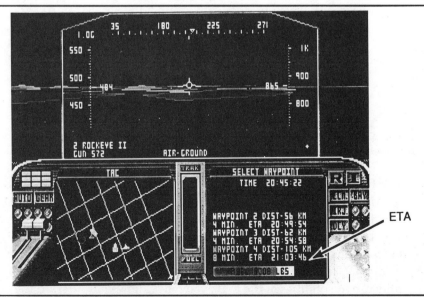

ETA

Figure 8-6.   Waypoint Display in right MFD with ETAs shown

you can be late. On most real fighter missions being late is not an option; if you see that you can't make it on time you usually have to abort the mission.

Revenge Belongs to God

General Patton once said "revenge belongs to God." He was speaking about getting emotionally involved in the fight and having it cloud your tactical perspective. Because of the realism of the simulation it is easy to get mad at the enemy and want to get even. When I first started flying the F-19 simulation, I took it personally any time the enemy shot at me. In fact, I still do. I have learned, however, to keep control of my emotions and execute my tactical game plan.

In the F-19 simulation there is a decided benefit to entering enemy territory "like a mouse" and coming out "like a lion." There are very few times when it pays to go out of your way to get even with the enemy. While flying in the simulation you should stay hidden, strike suddenly, and then disappear again. Only when you are discovered and engaged do you need to fight. While fighting the enemy, you should constantly be thinking about slipping back into a concealed position as soon as the opportunity presents itself.

THE RACE GOES ON

The F-19 simulation represents the modern day battlefield where Stealth aircraft such as the F-19 have a definite technical advantage over an enemy heavily dependent on radar defenses. It is still up to you, however, to use this technical superiority to gain victory. Air combat history is full of descriptions of air battles won by superior pilots flying inferior aircraft (Claire Chenault's Flying Tigers are one of the best examples). In order to fully use the abilities of the F-19, you must know your aircraft, the enemy, and yourself. Hopefully this book has helped you with all three of these.

The F-19 simulation provides the pilot with a window into the future to view and experience the effect of Stealth technology on a future war. Just remember that technological leads are very transitory in nature. While aircraft may now have the upper hand, it will not be long before the defenders catch up with an entirely new system. No matter how high we raise the technological stakes, "the race goes on." For better or worse you can always count on one thing when it comes to air combat technology — the race will always go on.

Index

The Best of Times

America's hot new best-seller takes you on a trip through the golden age of railroading in America and Europe. Compete with famous rail barons. Plan, build, operate, maintain and expand your railroad into a mighty industrial machine.

1990 brings phenomenal new graphics and game play to the World War II submarine game that won Simulation of the Year honors around the world in 1986. Stalk Japanese ships through the Pacific from Pearl Harbor to VJ Day.

The Software Publishers Association named this one Simulation of the Year. Engrossing game play. Fascinating strategies. Revolutionary graphics. Based on America's radar-elusive jet.

Command not just one tank, but a full platoon of four with controls so smooth they put single-tank games to shame. Call in jets, helicopters, artillery and infantry support, too.

Dogfighting is the name of this game. No experience? No problem: just turn on all the rookie options and you'll be up to your eyeballs in dazzling graphics and furious fun.

Discover the game that has the critics raving. Fight and scheme your way to power and prestige in a role-playing/action/adventure of war and politics in 16th Century Japan.

Take on shrewd Russian commanders in a gripping game of nuclear submarine strategy. Find and destroy the enemy with the latest sonar and weapons. Based on Tom Clancy's novel.

Join The MicroProse Squadron and Win Great Prizes!

Can't find these games? Call 1-800-879-PLAY for prices and ordering information. ©1990 MicroProse Software, Inc. All Rights Reserved.

**The Best of Times
All the Time.**